OLD TESTAMENT
SINNERS AND SAINTS

Discover What These 100 Intriguing
Bible Characters Can Teach Us Today

PETER DEHAAN

ISBNs:
        978-1-948082-73-0 (e-book)
        978-1-948082-74-7 (paperback)
        978-1-948082-75-4 (hardcover)

Library of Congress Control Number: 2022901118

Published by Rock Rooster Books, Grand Rapids, Michigan

Credits:
        Developmental editor: Kathryn Wilmotte
        Copy editor/proofreader: Robyn Mulder
        Cover design: Taryn Nergaard
        Author photo: Chelsie Jensen Photography

To Dan DeHaan

Books in the Bible Bios Series

- *Women of the Bible: The Victorious, the Victims, the Virtuous, and the Vicious*

- *The Friends and Foes of Jesus: Discover How People in the New Testament React to God's Good News*

- *Old Testament Sinners and Saints: Discover What These 100 Intriguing Bible Characters Can Teach Us Today*

Be the first to hear about Peter's new books and receive updates at PeterDeHaan.com/updates.

Contents

Part 5: Daniel, Prophet and Dream

Celebrating the Old Testament

Some Christians dismiss the Old Testament. They argue that since Jesus came to fulfill the Law and the Prophets (Matthew 5:17), what it says doesn't matter to them or their faith practices today. Other Christians embrace the Old Testament, putting it on an equal footing with the New Testament. They reason that all Scripture—both the Old and New Testaments—has merit (2 Timothy 3:16).

We should instead embrace the Old Testament for what it is and let it inform our understanding of the New Testament and the faith practices it reveals. We can most appreciate God's New Testament of Scripture from the foundation the Old Testament provides.

From this perspective, we can celebrate the Old Testament. It has two main purposes. The first is to reveal God to us. The second is to anticipate the coming Savior, Jesus.

In the Old Testament law—given to us through Moses—a mind-numbing list of things to do and not do confronts us. This is to make us right with Father God. But it's an impossible undertaking to achieve. Everyone falls short, whether by a little or a lot, it matters not. We all miss the mark of the Old Testament's prescription (James 2:10).

Yet the Old Testament also gives us hope of the coming Savior who will offer a better way for us to approach God. It's a way everyone can realize—if they want to. It's believing in Jesus and following him as his disciple. This is so much better than a bunch of impossible-to-keep rules.

In this way, we can best read and understand the Old Testament as it anticipates and points us toward Jesus, the Messiah.

From this perspective we'll explore one hundred characters of the Old Testament. These people appear in approximate chronological order, given that many of their stories overlap and others are hard to place on the biblical timeline. To provide perspective, we'll anchor our exploration of these people around five notable biblical characters: Adam, Abraham, Moses, David, and Daniel.

Some of these one hundred Old Testament characters provide examples to follow. We'll call these people saints, even though they're less than perfect. The Old Testament also includes a colorful list of screwups (sinners), the people who fall short and make a mess of things. We can see them as examples to avoid.

Several of these people share names with other biblical characters. For example, did you know there are two people named Noah in the Bible? Whenever we encounter a duplicate name, we'll add a number at the end to help us keep things straight. You can learn more about this in "Bonus Content: Duplicate Names" in the back of the book.

As we consider these individuals on a continuum from mostly good to mostly bad, remember that all of them miss the mark of meeting God's Old Testament expectations. This points us to God's better way through Jesus as revealed in the New Testament.

May these Old Testament sinners and saints inform us to embrace Jesus, either to become his disciple or to live as one.

How do you view the Old Testament? Who are some of your favorite Old Testament characters? Why?

[Discover more in Acts 17:11.]

PART 1:

ADAM AND EVE

Our story begins at creation, where God created man and woman in his own image. From them, all humanity follows. After beginning with creation's first couple and their family, we'll consider Noah and then Job, preparing us to move into the second section about Father Abraham and his family.

Adam

The first person we encounter in the Bible is Adam. And the first couple we see is Adam and Eve. Though we usually think of them as a pair, let's for a moment look at just Adam.

In the beginning, God creates us in his image, male and female. This means that Adam, as the first person, exists in God's image. So do we. Think about that.

God places Adam in the garden of Eden. It's an idyllic paradise, yet it's not an idle existence. That would be boring. Instead, God gives Adam work to do. He's to care for God's garden. By extension, we, too, should care for God's garden—his creation—today.

Yet Adam is also alone.

God, who exists in community—as Father, Son, and Holy Spirit—knows the importance of Adam having someone to spend time with, someone to journey with through life. So God creates Eve—also made in his image—as a counterpart to Adam.

Though many versions of the Bible refer to Eve as Adam's helper, I appreciate the translations which use words such as "partner," "companion," "complement," and "counterpart." In these we see a matched pair, equal to each other.

God gives Adam and Eve one rule: to not eat from one tree. All the rest of the garden's produce is for them to enjoy, all except for this one plant. This is because its fruit contains special power. It possesses the ability for the people who eat it to know right from wrong, to discern between good and evil.

One simple rule.

Yet Adam and Eve do the one thing God told them not to do. Enticed by the crafty serpent, they eat from the one tree—the only tree—God instructed them to not touch. Yet the ripened produce looks so good. Eve picks some and eats it. She gives some to Adam. They both eat the forbidden fruit.

When God confronts Adam, he blames Eve. Eve in turn blames the serpent. Yet each played a role, and God punishes all three.

Scripture later holds Adam accountable—mostly. It is through him that sin entered our world. It's because of him that we face death.

And this is where Jesus comes in. Because of Adam's sin we will die. Because of Jesus's sacrifice we can live.

Who do we blame more in this story, Adam, Eve, or the serpent? Does it matter whose fault it is?

Do you believe you can live because of Jesus? Do you have eternal life through him? (See John 3:14–17 for details.)

[Read Adam's story in Genesis 2–3. Discover more in 1 Corinthians 15:22.]

Eve

Eve is a well-known biblical figure. Surprisingly, she's only mentioned by name four times in the Bible, twice in Genesis and twice in the New Testament. Her name may mean "living," and we see her as the mother of humanity, with all future generations coming from her. But Eve is best known for picking the fruit God specifically prohibited and giving some to her husband. As a result of their sin, God expels them from the garden of Eden.

Though most of Scripture places the blame on Adam's shoulders, in one place Paul does implicate Eve (2 Corinthians 11:3), though we must be careful to not take this verse out of context.

Despite this, Eve often receives the harshest criticism for disobeying God. Adam, however, is equally guilty. He could have—and should have—put a stop to eating the forbidden fruit. He knew better. More contemptible is the serpent, who lied to seduce Eve into disobeying God. Because of their actions, all three—Adam, Eve, and the serpent—suffer consequences, which they pass on to future generations. This includes us.

Eve receives three punishments for her disobedience: pain in childbirth, a desire to control her husband, and him ruling over her. This suggests that before Adam and Eve messed up, we can assume things would have been the opposite for women: childbirth would have been easy, women would not seek to control their husbands, and men would not try to rule over their wives.

The judgment Eve receives transfers forward to future generations, with women trying to control men and men wanting to rule women. However, in the beginning there was neither controlling nor ruling. There is equality, with God intending that men and women live as equals.

In marriage, this doesn't mean wives merely helping their husbands but more so functioning as partners, companions, complements, and counterparts to each other.

We'll do well to apply this mindset to all our interactions with others, both male and female.

Do we try to control those around us? Do we let others rule over us? How might God want us to change?

[Read Eve's story in Genesis 2:18–4:1. Discover more in 1 Timothy 2:13–14.]

Cain

After Adam and Eve leave the garden of Eden, they have Cain. The Bible doesn't specifically say he's their firstborn, but he is the first of their offspring we read about in Scripture. Eve praises God for his role in this, the miracle of birth.

Later, Eve gives birth to Cain's younger brother, Abel. The boys grow up and begin to work: Cain as a farmer, Abel as a shepherd.

Cain and Abel both give the results of their labors as an offering to God. We don't know why they do this because the Almighty hadn't asked them to. This is well before Moses commands the people to give God offerings and sacrifices. Nevertheless, the boys desire to give back to God.

Perhaps Cain decides to go first, and Abel simply follows his older brother's example.

God accepts Abel's gift but not Cain's. We don't know why.

One thought is that while Cain offered *some* of his crops to God, Abel offered the firstborn from his flock, the best. Another idea is that this foreshadows the law of Moses and ultimately the sacrifice of Jesus, which requires the shedding of blood (Hebrews 9:22). Abel's offering could accomplish this; Cain's could not. Or there may be another explanation we're unaware of.

Regardless, God affirms Abel but not Cain. Imagine giving something to God and having him reject it. We can understand why Cain was angry and upset.

Still, God speaks to Cain and encourages him to do what is right. Sin knocks on Cain's door. It desires to control him. God tells Cain to rule over the temptation.

As you may know, Cain doesn't.

He invites his brother out into the field. There he attacks his younger sibling and kills him. We don't know if Cain intended to murder his brother, but the story does read as though Cain premeditated the attack. The outcome of death may have been deliberate or accidental.

Either way, Abel dies. And Cain is the world's first murderer.

God punishes Cain for his sin and drives him away.

Two brothers. One dead and the other exiled. What a sad outcome for creation's first family.

What can we do to get along better with our brothers and sisters? When we face the temptation to sin, what must we do to control it and not give in to it?

[Read Cain's story in Genesis 4:1–24. Discover more in Hebrews 11:4 and 1 John 3:12.]

Abel

Having discussed Cain, we now know the story of Abel, Adam and Eve's second child. To recap, Abel and Cain give gifts to God. The Almighty accepts Abel's gift but not Cain's. Cain is angry and kills Abel.

Though we can speculate why God approved Abel's offering and not Cain's, we don't know for sure—at least not from the account in Genesis.

The book of Hebrews, however, gives us a clue. One passage outlines the faith of many of the Bible's heroes. Among them we read of Abel.

Hebrews says that by faith Abel offered a better sacrifice than Cain. Furthermore, it says that because of faith, God praised his gift and affirmed Abel as righteous. The implication is that Abel received God's affirmation with a humble spirit and didn't let it go to his head. In short, Abel kept his ego in check.

Though we might expect God to then protect Abel for his noteworthy faith, remember that Cain had the ability to determine his actions. The only way for God to stop Cain would be to take away his free will.

How hard it must've been for God to not intervene and prevent Cain from killing his brother. Yet
it's not in his nature to stop us from doing something
we want to do—even if it's something quite terrible.
This is a result from living in a sin-filled world.

Though Cain cuts Abel's life short, we can expect Abel's faith brings him into God's presence right
away. What a wonderful outcome.

*How strong is our faith? Does God commend us for giv-
ing him our best, through faith? Do we respond with a
faith-driven humility when he affirms us?*

[Read about Abel in Genesis 4:1–24. Discover more
in Hebrews 11:4.]

Noah (1)

Following the biblical story arc, we move forward several generations. Sin entered the world through Adam, found its expression in Cain, and, over the following centuries, chaos prevails. The world becomes corrupt, filled with violence.

God decides to wipe away humanity's rampant evil.

The rest of God's creation can stay, but he decides to do away with people—all except for Noah and his family. The Bible calls Noah righteous. This means he lives rightly, even though God has not yet defined what that means. Noah is blameless in his life and walks faithfully with God.

Scripture doesn't tell us the spiritual condition of Noah's family: his wife, his three sons, and their wives. These seven may be righteous like Noah, but the Bible doesn't say that. Regardless, God plans to save all eight. A better understanding is that they will live not because of their own merit but because of Noah's. So it is with us and Jesus.

God plans to send a massive flood to destroy the world. Only these eight people will survive. Everyone else will die. Most land animals will perish as innocent victims in all this. Then God will allow humanity to start anew, through Noah. It's a massive do-over, Creation 2.0.

To accomplish this, God tells Noah to build an ark, a huge boat, one big enough to carry a representative pair of each species and seven pairs of clean animals—along with enough food for all.

Noah obeys.

People back then lived for several centuries, and it takes Noah and his family one hundred years to complete this massive project. Building an ark doesn't make sense and requires years of backbreaking work. Yet they persist, no doubt enduring the ridicule of those around them and making many sacrifices as they build God's boat, all the while attending to the daily needs of living.

When the rains come and the floodwaters rise, Noah, his family, and the animals God sends to them board the ark. God seals them inside and they survive the great deluge.

When the waters recede, eight people emerge.

God then gives Noah the same command he gave Adam and Eve, to be fruitful and multiply. They do. We're here today as a result.

God told Noah to do something difficult that didn't make sense from a human perspective. But Noah obeyed and saved his family, along with giving humanity a fresh start.

We applaud Noah for his obedience to God.

How well do we do at obeying God? Would we be obedient like Noah if God told us to undertake a huge task that would take several years to complete?

[Read about Noah in Genesis 5:28–9:29. Discover more in Hebrews 11:7.]

Shem

The Bible doesn't tell us the name of Noah's wife, but we do know the names of their three sons: Shem, Ham, and Japheth.

Scripture says Noah obeyed God in building the ark. We can only assume his boys helped. If they didn't, why would God allow them to enter the ark and live?

After the flood, Noah, a farmer, plants a vineyard. He makes some wine, gets drunk, and lounges around without his clothes. Hearing this, Shem and his brother Japheth modestly cover their father, without looking at his nakedness.

When Noah sobers, he blesses Shem and Japheth for their chaste action, specifically elevating Shem over his brothers.

As we read the family tree of Shem, we come across Abram, later called Abraham. Through Shem's lineage we have Father Abraham and, much later, Jesus.

How can we be an example to do what is right? When we see someone doing what's wrong, do we seek to make things better?

[Read about Shem and his brothers in Genesis 9:18–27. Discover Shem's family tree in Genesis 11:10–26.]

Ham

Of Noah's three sons, the Bible lists Ham second, even though he is, in fact, the youngest. Scripture only gives us one story about him. It's his role in the account of his father's drunken stupor.

It's Ham who discovers his father inebriated and naked. He could have discreetly covered his dad. He doesn't. Instead, he tells his brothers. Though we don't know Ham's motives, we doubt he seeks their advice on what to do. More likely he approaches them with the glee of a gossip, sharing the tantalizing tidbits of what dear old dad has done. In short, he's laughing at his father and expecting his brothers to join him.

While Ham does nothing to help alleviate his dad's situation and prevent future embarrassment, brothers Shem and Japheth do both.

When Noah sobers and learns what happened, he blesses Shem and Japheth for their proper response but not before cursing Ham. We don't know why, but Noah directs his displeasure at Ham's son Canaan, pronouncing Canaan will be the lowest of slaves to his brothers. And later, while blessing Japheth, Noah specifically proclaims Canaan will be the slave of Japheth. This makes us wonder if Canaan wasn't also involved in his father Ham's folly.

Ham has four sons. In addition to Canaan, he has Cush, Egypt, and Put. From Canaan we have the Canaanites, a recurring irritant to God's chosen people, the Israelites, who descend from Canaan's uncle Shem.

The only other reference we see of Ham occurs in Psalms, where it talks about the tents of Ham and the land of Ham, presumably where some of Ham's descendants settled.

Whether we're the youngest in our family or not, what can we do to rise above our station to act with integrity? When we see someone's misfortune are we quick to tell others about it (gossip) or do we keep it to ourselves?

[Read about Ham and his brothers in Genesis 9:18–27. Discover Ham's family tree in Genesis 10:6–20.]

Japheth

We've covered Noah's sons Shem and Ham. Now we'll look at the third, Japheth. Of the three boys, the Bible tells us the least about Japheth, though we know that Japheth, along with Shem, acts with integrity to cover his father's drunken nakedness. And we know that Noah blesses Japheth for his action.

That's it.

Though Scripture gives us Japheth's family tree, it's a brief one, shorter than the lists of his brothers' lineage. In scanning the record of Japheth's descendants, no familiar names pop up. As far as the biblical account is concerned, Japheth and his family disappear from its pages.

What can we do to live a life that honors God? What can we do to encourage our descendants to do the same thing and, as a result, preserve our lineage for God's glory?

[Read about Japheth and his brothers in Genesis 9:18–27. Discover Japheth's family tree in Genesis 10:2–5.]

Job

We don't know when Job lived, but many Bible scholars consider him a contemporary of Abraham. This places Job several generations after Noah in our biblical timeline.

Job lives in the land of Uz. We know four key things about him:

First, he is a righteous man, acting justly in all he does and conducting himself with blame-free confidence. He puts God first and avoids evil.

Next, Job is a family man. He and his wife have ten children, a quiver full (Psalm 127:5), which people see as a sign of God's favor.

Third, Job is concerned for his kids and their future. After they have a party, he offers a burnt offering sacrifice for each one of them to purify them of any sin or careless thought. He wants to help make them right with God.

Last, Job is rich. He owns over 10,000 animals, with a large staff to oversee his herds. He is the wealthiest man in the area and esteemed by all.

As such, Job enjoys an idyllic life of ease with favor from God. Everyone looks up to him, and Job's life seems perfect.

Yet Satan seeks to torment Job. Though God gives Satan permission to act, God isn't the cause of Job's suffering, Satan is. Don't forget that.

Satan strips away Job's wealth and kills his children. Then Satan attacks Job's health, leaving him clinging to life with an unsupportive wife. But in all this Job remains faithful to God.

Job perseveres through these afflictions and doesn't buckle under his friends' less-than-helpful advice, as we'll see in the following four chapters.

Eventually, God rewards Job for his faithfulness by restoring his health, returning his wealth times two, and giving him ten more children. Job lives another 140 years, celebrating life with his children, grandchildren, great-grandchildren, and great-great-grandchildren.

When unthinkable hardship afflicts us, how can we remain steadfast in our devotion to God? When it seems everyone and everything is against us, will we continue to put God first?

[Read Job's story in the book of Job, especially Job 1, 2, and 42. Discover more in Ezekiel 14:13–14 and 9–20.]

Learn even more about Job and his friends in the devotional Bible study *I Hope in Him: 40 Insights about
Moving from Despair to Deliverance through the Life
of Job,* which explores this classic story as a mod-
ern-day screenplay.

Eliphaz (1)

Job has three friends, Eliphaz, Bildad, and Zophar, who hear of his plight and come to offer sympathy and comfort. The sight of his suffering appalls them, and they barely recognize their friend. They weep for his condition, tearing their clothes as a sign of mourning, and sprinkling dust on their heads to show their sorrow. They say nothing for several days.

These three men don't appear elsewhere in the Bible, so we know little about them, except for what they say to their struggling friend.

Each takes their turn in offering a series of monologues to Job, but as we'll see, they fall short in offering him sympathy and comfort.

Eliphaz the Temanite is the first to speak. He might go first because he is the oldest. Or the wealthiest. Or the wisest. Or perhaps he's simply bolder than his two friends.

Eliphaz has had a long time to consider what he'll say to Job. Though his words could have offered comfort to his suffering friend, instead they come out as an accusation, judging Job for presumed shortcomings.

Eliphaz doesn't know Job's heart, and he certainly lacks an understanding of God's perspective, but Eliphaz speaks as though he knows both. We might wonder if his critical words are more directed to himself than to Job.

Then his two friends follow him with their own speeches. After hearing them speak, Eliphaz tries a second time. Instead of correcting the errors of his first diatribe, he doubles down. He persists in the notion that the hardship Job endured stands as a confirmation of Job's evil heart and a mark of God's disapproval. But Eliphaz speaks through arrogance and ignorance. His view of God is incomplete, so his conclusions fall short. And when he casts his flawed logic on Job, he inflicts unnecessary pain on his friend.

For his third and final speech, Eliphaz claims our relationship with God is transactional. He assumes that if we behave right, then God will bless us. And if we do what is wrong, God will punish us. Eliphaz sees Job's situation as God's punishment, concluding that Job suffers because of his sins.

Thankfully, this isn't how God treats his people.

How can we make sure our words help others and don't cause pain? When things go wrong, do we view it as God's punishment, whether on ourselves or on others?

[Read what Eliphaz says in Job 4, 15, and 22. Discover more in Job 2:11 and 42:7.]

Bildad

The second man in Job's trio of friends is Bildad the Shuhite. Like Eliphaz, Bildad also offers Job three speeches.

In his first oration, Bildad looks at Job's situation and assumes he received what he deserves. Bildad equates right living with God's favor and hardship with sin and God's displeasure. While this certainly can be the case, it isn't absolute, which is hard for many people to accept. It doesn't seem fair.

When he speaks a second time, Bildad assumes he knows the truth and Job is in error, since his life is on track and Job's isn't. Bildad thinks his prosperity gives him the right to speak, and Job's misery requires him to listen. But high status does not make us wise. Though Bildad thinks he has something worthwhile to say, he is wrong. His words shoot forth as arrows, inflicting hurt as well as failing to help.

In his final and shortest speech, Bildad gives Job something to think about. Between worshiping God for who he is and acknowledging we are nothing next to him, Bildad asks, "How can a mere mortal be worthy to stand before the Almighty God?"

From our perspective today we know that by ourselves we can't, but through Jesus we can. Thank you, Jesus.

What can we do to make sure the words we say build people up and don't tear them down? How do we view our relationship with God?

[Read what Bildad says in Job 8, 18, and 25. Discover more in Job 2:11 and 42:7.]

Zophar

Zophar the Naamathite is the third of Job's friends to speak. But unlike them, he only talks twice. Might he have realized that their words were only causing their friend distress? Could he have concluded that, sometimes, saying nothing is better than saying something?

In his first monologue, Zophar says that Job thinks his beliefs are flawless. Ironically, Zophar acts the same way about his. Like his two friends, Zophar does nothing to offer Job comfort or clarity. Instead, Zophar uses the logic of an incomplete theology to conclude Job is suffering so much because he has sinned.

The second time Zophar speaks, he shares his view that God always punishes the wicked, making them suffer for what they've done. Zophar concludes by saying that Job's deep suffering confirms he's an especially wicked man.

Do we equate suffering with divine punishment? How can we use our words to help people rather than hurt them?

[Read what Zophar says in Job 11 and 20. Discover more in Job 2:11 and 42:7.]

Elihu (1)

Aside from the three friends Eliphaz, Bildad, and Zophar, we also encounter a fourth man on the scene, Elihu, son of Barakel. The Bible doesn't say if he came with the three others or arrived later. But Scripture does say he defers to them because they're older. He does this as a sign of respect.

Though Elihu only speaks once, his rant is by far the longest.

He starts by responding to Job's claim that though he calls out to God, there's no answer. Elihu says God speaks through dreams, visions, circumstances, and audible words, even through angels. It's up to us to perceive his message. If Job isn't hearing, it must be his fault.

In Elihu's limited understanding of God, he perceives the Almighty as one who fairly administers justice but nothing more. But we're frail people, we do wrong. We sin. If God *only* administers justice, then he must punish us for *all* our mistakes.

As Elihu continues to speak, we see him arrogantly proclaim that he has the knowledge his friends lack. He repeats his view of God's justice and implies Job is receiving the punishment he deserves.

How does God speak to us? Are we open to hear from him regardless of how he reveals himself? Have we accepted the solution Jesus offers as an alternative to the justice we deserve?

[Read what Elihu says in Job 32:6–37:24.]

Job's Daughters

After Satan torments the innocent Job, God restores what the enemy took away.

God doubles Job's wealth and gives him ten more children: seven sons and three daughters. Though the Bible doesn't mention the boys' names, Scripture records the names of Job's daughters: Jemimah, Keziah, and Keren-Happuch. The girls are the most beautiful women in the land.

In mentioning them by name, the Bible honors Job's girls, even at the risk of elevating them over their unnamed brothers. More so, Job goes against the conventional practice of the day, giving his daughters an inheritance along with their brothers. He treats them fairly, as equals.

In doing so, Job reveals both his heart and God's perspective. Given that Job lives in a male-dominated society, his decision to treat his girls as equal to their brothers is even more remarkable. In doing so, Job shows us that just because everyone else does something doesn't mean we should—or that it's right.

How can we better see things as God sees them? What might we do to further God's perspective, even if it means challenging the status quo?

[Read about Job's three daughters in Job 42:13–15.]

PART 2:

FATHER ABRAHAM

Our next group of biblical characters focuses on Abraham and his next two generations. They provide the foundation for God's chosen people: the Hebrew race and the nation of Israel. But before we get to Abraham, we need some background first, so we'll start with Terah.

Terah

The Bible tells us that Terah is the eighth generation from Noah's son Shem. So our story picks up a couple of centuries after Noah and the great flood. Terah has three sons, Abram, Nahor (2), and Haran. Haran dies at the start of our story, but not before he has a son, Lot, Terah's grandson and Abram's nephew.

Though the Bible doesn't tell us why, Terah decides to go to Canaan, which is a long journey. He takes with him his son Abram, Abram's wife Sarai, and his grandson Lot. He leaves behind his other son, Nahor, Nahor's wife, and most likely some grandchildren.

Though they head for Canaan, the troop never makes it there. Midway on their trip, Terah aborts his journey. He stops at Harran and settles there instead of Canaan, his original destination.

Terah dies in Harran, leaving Abram, Sarai, and Lot to figure out what to do next.

Traveling to Canaan represented a long journey for Terah and his family. Though we can later infer that God had his hand in this ambitious move, it's only speculation.

What we do know is that Terah had a plan but gave up before he completed it.

Are we known for not following through with our plans? When we say we'll do something, do others have confidence that we'll do it?

[Read Terah's story in Genesis 11:24–32. Discover more in Joshua 24:2.]

Abram/Abraham

While living in Harran, God comes to Abram and tells him to go to the land he will show him. Abram obeys, setting out from Harran when he's seventy-five years old. He takes his wife Sarai and nephew Lot, along with the possessions they acquired while living in Harran. They head for Canaan. The Bible doesn't explicitly state Canaan to be the place God shows him, but we can assume this is the case.

Interestingly, Canaan is where Abram's father Terah had originally headed to when he stopped midjourney to live in Harran instead. This leads us to wonder if God had originally called Terah to Canaan, a mission Abram had to finish after his father failed to complete it.

Upon arriving in Canaan—an act of obedience—Abram's real story begins. His life stands as an inspiring journey with God. It's a faith-filled adventure, with a few hiccups along the way. Yet he perseveres and God esteems his faith.

One of the pivotal junctures in Abram's life occurs when God forms an everlasting covenant with Abram when he is ninety-nine years old. The Almighty affirms Abram's faithful walk with him and calls him blameless. What an astounding affirmation.

God also promises to make him the father of many nations, even though he has no children. At this point, God changes his name from Abram to Abraham. Abram means "exalted father" and Abraham means "father of many." This name change represents an expanded scope, despite Abraham having no offspring—yet.

The phrase "Father Abraham" reflects both his old name and new. It appears several times in both the Old and New Testaments of the Bible.

Another notable aspect of Abraham's life is the idea of God blessing him to bless others. The ultimate form of this blessing comes through Abraham's descendant Jesus, who dies as the once-and-for-all sacrifice to make us right with Father God.

This idea of being blessed to be a blessing to others is a vision we can all follow. God blesses us so we can bless others.

There's much more to share about Abraham's life. We'll cover key aspects in the next several chapters.

Would God esteem us for our faith? How well do we do at blessing others when God blesses us?

[Read about Abram in Genesis 11:26–17:4, and read about Abraham in Genesis 17:5–25:11. Discover more in Acts 3:25; Romans 4:1–3; and James 2:20–24.]

Lot

We don't know how old Lot is when his father dies, but his grandfather, Terah, appears to take him in. We can assume this because when Terah heads out for Canaan, he takes grandson Lot with him, along with son Abram, and daughter-in-law Sarai.

When Terah dies, Abram travels on to Canaan, taking Lot with him. The trio of Abram, Sarai, and Lot travel together, but seeing how Lot's story unfolds, he may have been better off staying behind.

The first glimpse into Lot's character comes after Abram's and Lot's herdsmen fight over grazing land. The pair decide to separate themselves and their flocks. Being the oldest, the choice belongs to Abram, but he lets Lot pick. Lot takes the best land for himself and leaves the subpar area for his uncle.

Later Lot moves to the city of Sodom, which God decides to destroy for their sinfulness. God tells his plan to Abram, now called Abraham. Abraham lobbies God for mercy, but God doesn't waver in his decision. He does, however, provide a rescue for Lot and his family, sending two angels to extract them prior to the city's destruction.

When the angels arrive, the men in the city want to have sex with them. Lot tries to intervene, offering them his daughters instead. What a horrifying decision. What does this teach Lot's daughters about their value? Fortunately for them, the men aren't interested. Lot tries his best to rescue the angels from the men, but the visitors end up rescuing Lot instead.

With time running out, the angels drag Lot, his wife, and their two daughters from the city. As God's destruction falls upon Sodom, Lot's fleeing wife looks back to see what she's leaving behind. She dies instantly.

This leaves Lot with his two daughters. Fearing for their safety, they end up living in a cave. With their biological clocks ticking and no men in sight, the girls conspire to get their father drunk and sleep with him on successive nights. Lot impregnates them both, and they each have boys. This is the last we hear of Lot.

The life of Lot serves as a tale of what to avoid. We see him as a selfish man who lacks integrity and does what's best for himself. He's also a poor father who fails to raise godly daughters, disregarding their purity and diminishing their value. It's no wonder they have no reservation in seducing him to produce children for them.

Do we make self-centered decisions that reveal a lack of integrity? Are we doing all we can to raise godly children and positively influence those around us?

[Read Lot's story in Genesis 11:27–14:16 and 19:1–38. Discover more in 2 Peter 2:4–9.]

Sarai/Sarah (1)

The story of Sarai, later called Sarah, intersperses throughout the narrative of Genesis 11–23. She is the first wife of Abraham and is also his half-sister. Though this thought makes us squirm today, at the time—prior to God giving his laws to Moses—a man marrying his half-sister isn't taboo.

Sarah, whose name means *princess*, is most attractive. Abraham worries that would-be suitors will kill him to get her, so he asks her to say she is his sister—which is half true. He even claims this will be an act of love.

She agrees and does so—twice—allowing other men to take her as their wife. Both times God protects her and works out her return to Abraham, but what torment she must go through when they take her away, and Abraham does nothing to stop them.

Although God repeatedly promises Abraham children, Sarah remains barren. She grows impatient waiting for the Almighty to act. Taking God's promise upon herself, she devises a plan for Abraham to have his promised child through her servant, Hagar. It's an ill-conceived idea, and Abraham is foolish for agreeing to take part. As we will see in upcoming chapters, conflict results.

Later God confirms Abraham's chosen child will come from Sarah. She laughs at this improbable promise, and God criticizes her for it. A year later, the child is born when Sarah is ninety and Abraham is one hundred. They name him Isaac, which means *laughter* or *he laughs.*

Sarah lives another thirty-seven years and dies at age 127.

With God, all things are possible, even a ninety-year-old woman having a baby or living for 127 years.

Have we ever grown tired of waiting for God to act? In our impatience have we ever tried to do things our own way?

[Read about Sarai in Genesis 11:29–31 and 16:1–6, and read about Sarah in Genesis 17:15–18:15 and 20:1–21:13. Discover more in Hebrews 11:11.]

Hagar

Hagar is the Egyptian slave of Sarah (Sarai), likely acquired on Abraham and Sarah's trip to Egypt during a famine. They could have avoided so much pain had they not bought her—or used better judgment afterward. Here's her story.

Sarah has no children, which she blames on God. She's well past her childbearing years. In desperation, she offers her slave, Hagar, to Abraham to make a baby. Sarah reasons she can vicariously have the family God promised her through Hagar.

This is a poor idea on Sarah's part, yet Abraham accepts it without reservation.

Hagar becomes pregnant by Abraham. Though the pair never marry, the Bible later refers to Hagar as Abraham's wife. Being able to give Abraham what Sarah could not, Hagar looks down on Sarah, who blames Abraham for the whole mess. Wanting to avoid conflict, Abraham tells Sarah to deal with the problem herself.

Sarah mistreats Hagar, who runs away. Alone in the desert, God's angel sends Hagar back to Sarah, promising that her descendants will one day be too numerous to count. Hagar obeys God, and soon Ishmael is born.

For the next fourteen years, life with Abraham and Sarah is okay for Hagar and Ishmael, but then Sarah becomes pregnant in her old age and gives birth to Isaac. Now Abraham has two sons from different moms.

Ishmael taunts his younger half-brother, Isaac.

Again, Sarah demands that Abraham fix the problem. This troubles Abraham, but God tells him to do as Sarah requested, for Abraham's legacy will come through Isaac, not Ishmael.

Abraham sends Hagar and Ishmael off with some food and water. When their supplies are gone, they sit down in the wilderness to die.

But God hasn't forgotten them, and he promises Hagar that her son will become a great nation. Then the Lord shows her water.

Hagar is a powerless victim. She has no say over what Abraham and Sarah do to her. Even so, God protects her. He cares for her, and through Ishmael, her descendants are numerous and become a great nation (Genesis 17:20).

What can we do to help the powerless? When we're mistreated, will we trust God with our future?

[Read Hagar's story in Genesis 16:1–15 and 21:8–19. Discover more in Galatians 4:21–26.]

Ishmael (1)

Ishmael is the oldest son of Abraham and Hagar, Sarah's slave. Though this might make Ishmael a slave as well, Abraham treats him as a son. When God promises Abraham that he'll be the father of many nations, he gives Abraham the rite of circumcision. Abraham circumcises Ishmael according to God's command.

When Ishmael is fourteen, Sarah—who is effectively his stepmother—gets pregnant. She gives Abraham his second son, Isaac. This makes Ishmael and Isaac half-brothers.

Ishmael mocks his much younger brother.

This distresses Sarah, who insists Abraham get rid of Hagar and her impudent son. This will ensure that Isaac will not have to share his inheritance with his older half-brother.

This deeply troubles Abraham, who loves Ishmael, his firstborn. But God tells Abraham to not let Sarah's request upset him, to do what she asked. The Lord's promised blessings for Abraham will come through Isaac. Even so, a nation will also come from Ishmael.

The next day Abraham sends Hagar and Ishmael away.

They wander into the desert. With their provisions gone, Hagar sits down and cries. But God comes to her, provides comfort, and shows her water. Like he did with Abraham, God promises Hagar that he will make her son, Ishmael, into a great nation.

The pair survive. Hagar, an Egyptian, gets an Egyptian wife for her son.

Many years later, when Abraham dies, Ishmael and Isaac bury him. This shows his two sons have reconciled. But we don't know if it's just for this moment or a more lasting connection.

Ishmael has twelve sons, who become twelve tribal leaders. This implies the birth of a nation, just as God promised to both Abraham and Hagar. Ishmael dies at the age of 137.

What can we do to reconnect with estranged relatives or former friends? Do we believe God's promises to us will come true?

[Read Ishmael's story in Genesis 16:9–17 and 21:8–21. Discover more in Genesis 25:8–10.]

Isaac

Isaac is a child of older parents—much older. His mother, Sarah, is ninety when Isaac is born. And her husband Abraham is one hundred. At this advanced age, it seems impossible to have a child, yet through God all things are possible. From a human standpoint, we call Isaac's arrival a miracle—a miracle conception and a miracle birth.

Though Isaac is Sarah's only son, he has an older half-brother, Ishmael. But Abraham and Sarah send Ishmael and his mother away after Isaac is born.

With Ishmael no longer in the picture, God deems Isaac as Abraham's only son (Genesis 22:2, 12, and 16).

God tells Abraham to do the unthinkable, to sacrifice his boy as a burnt offering. Though this is something other gods demand of their people—and God will later tell Moses that human sacrifice is unacceptable– since God can raise Isaac from the dead, it's not out of the question for God to tell Abraham to kill his son. Even so, it's a horrific request.

Abraham intends to do exactly what God commanded. With the altar built and Isaac bound and lying atop it, Abraham raises his knife to kill his son—his one and only son—the son he dearly loves.

At this point, God stops Abraham from plunging the dagger into his son's chest. It was just a test, and Abraham passed. This proves that though Abraham loves his son much, he loves God even more.

Yet let's not look at this story only from Abraham's perspective but also from young Isaac's. His father is willing to kill him and nearly does.

This isn't something a child would ever forget. Not only would this surely scar Isaac in his relationship with his father, but it could also make him wary of the God behind it.

Would Isaac ever trust his father again? Would Isaac ever be able to trust God? We wouldn't blame Isaac if he turned his back on both his father and God. Yet Isaac sticks around. He doesn't reject his father, and he doesn't reject God. This is a tribute to Isaac's character.

This story serves as an encouragement to us that, regardless of our past, we can rise above it and not let it define who we become. Though things could have happened that we might want to blame on God, we can still trust him with our future and with our life.

Let's take a step back from the story. This isn't the only time the Bible talks about a father sacrificing his one and only son. Centuries later, Father God sacrifices his one and only son, Jesus. In doing so he proves his deep love for us. God wants to save us so we can be in a right relationship with him.

Our Heavenly Father sacrifices his one and only son to serve as the ultimate sacrifice to end all sacrifices for all the things all people have done throughout all time.

It's a gift of eternal life. All we need to do is accept it.

Has God ever asked us to do something that seemed too big or too hard? Could we sacrifice our child, as God later did with his?

More importantly, do we follow Jesus, God's sacrificed son, as our Lord and Savior?

[Read Isaac's story in Genesis 21–22 and 26–28. Discover more in Genesis 17:19–21 and Hebrews 11:17–19.]

Rebekah

Rebekah's family line is twisted. She's the daughter-in-law of Abraham and Sarah, as well as their great niece. (She is the daughter of their nephew Bethuel.) As a result, Rebekah's great aunt and uncle also become her in-laws when she marries their son Isaac.

Here's how it happens.

Abraham is adamant that his son Isaac should not marry a local girl. For this reason, he sends his servant back to where he grew up to find a bride for Isaac from among his own people.

God blesses the mission of Abraham's servant, directing him to meet Rebekah and confirming she is the one for Isaac when she offers to water the servant's camels. Rebekah agrees to go with him to marry a man she has never met. This is a tribute to her character.

Though we don't know Rebekah's age, Isaac is forty.

Just like Sarah, her mother-in-law, Rebekah is beautiful. And just like Abraham, Isaac later passes her off as his sister. This is an ill-conceived idea Isaac picked up from his parents.

Another parallel between Rebekah and Sarah is that both were childless for a long time. Rebekah and Isaac try for twenty years to have children. When she finally gets pregnant, she has twins.

Rebekah favors the younger, Jacob, while Isaac favors the older, Esau. Parents shouldn't play favorites. The outcome is never good.

The boys don't get along, likely driven by each parent preferring one son over the other. As a result, the twins live in conflict. When Esau threatens to kill Jacob, Rebekah feigns that she doesn't want Jacob to marry a local girl, hoping Isaac will send him back to their homeland. He does.

Rebekah is a beautiful woman of noble character. But she—along with her husband—isn't the best parent.

May we not repeat her mistakes.

What less-than-ideal character traits have we picked up from our parents? If we have children, are we serving as the best role model we can?

[Read Rebekah's story in Genesis 24–27. Discover more in Romans 9:10–13.]

Esau

Esau is the oldest of Isaac and Rebekah's twins. His father loves him, while his mother loves his younger brother, Jacob. Esau, also called Edom, will later become the father of a people called the Edomites.

The Bible records two key stories about Esau, neither of which works out well for him.

Esau grows up to be an accomplished hunter who loves the open country. One day after a long hunting expedition, Esau comes home famished. He smells the stew his younger brother, Jacob, is cooking.

"Quick, give me something to eat," Esau says.

Jacob doesn't. He sees an opportunity to best his older brother. "I'll give you a taste if you sell me your birthright." (A birthright is additional rights given to the firstborn son.)

"I'm starving," Esau replies. "What good is a birthright if I'm dead?"

He pledges his birthright to his brother and Jacob gives him food. Scripture concludes the story by confirming that Esau despised his birthright and the privileges of being the oldest brother.

If Esau is merely hungry when he asks Jacob for food, then selling his birthright as a quick way to fill his belly is indeed foolish. However, if Esau is dying from hunger, then he may indeed have easily given up his rights as the oldest son so that he may live.

Regardless, Jacob selfishly withholds food from his brother so he might usurp his brother's position as the firstborn.

Our second story of Esau comes much later. Isaac is old and nearing the end of his life. He wants to bless Esau before he dies. But first he asks Esau to hunt some game and prepare his favorite meal for him. Excited, Esau heads out.

Rebekah overhears this and concocts a plan for Jacob, her favorite son, to trick his blind father into giving him the blessing instead of his brother. Her scheme works and Isaac blesses Jacob, thinking he's blessing Esau instead. To accomplish this, Jacob first misleads and then lies to his father.

Esau's incensed when he finds out. Though his father blesses him as well, Isaac has already proclaimed the best blessings on Jacob and has little left for Esau.

Esau begrudges Jacob for taking his birthright and his blessing. Esau's anger simmers. He plans to kill his brother after Isaac dies.

If we struggle with family relationships, what can we do to repair them? How can we better appreciate the family God gave us?

[Read Esau's story in Genesis 25:24–34; 27:1–28:9; and 32:1–33:17. Discover more in Hebrews 12:16.]

Laban

After Rebekah learns of Esau's intent to kill Jacob—her favorite of the twins—she tells him to flee to his uncle Laban—her brother—to wait there until Esau's anger subsides.

Telling Isaac she doesn't want Jacob to marry a local girl, she gets her husband to agree to send Jacob away, thereby distancing him from Esau and his deadly threats.

Isaac and Rebekah send Jacob to Laban to marry one of his uncle's daughters, his first cousin. Though this makes us uncomfortable today, remember, it isn't until God gives his laws to Moses that he prohibits marrying a close relative.

Jacob heads east and finds his uncle. Laban has two daughters, Leah and Rachel. Jacob falls in love with the younger sister, Rachel, and agrees to work for his uncle for seven years in exchange for her.

The seven years fly by for Jacob, and soon Laban prepares the wedding. But the morning after, Jacob discovers he's married to Leah instead of Rachel. Laban has tricked him, but he defends himself by claiming their tradition holds that the older daughter must marry before the younger one can.

Laban then gives Rachel to Jacob as a second wife, but only if Jacob will agree to work for his father-in-law for another seven years.

We can sympathize with Jacob because Laban tricked him into marrying a woman he doesn't love and forced him to work an additional seven years to marry the woman he does. Laban doesn't treat Jacob with integrity. Even if Laban intended Leah to marry first, he should've told Jacob this right away and not seven years later when it was too late.

Yet we also realize that Jacob lacked integrity in dealing with his brother and his father. Might Jacob have treated Uncle Laban the same way? This might explain (but not justify) why Laban dealt shrewdly with Jacob.

Jacob then works six more years for Laban. This time his wages are a flock of his own. After twenty years of toiling for his father-in-law, God tells Jacob it's time to return home. Jacob heads out with his wives, many children, and flocks to return to the land God promised to give to Abraham. But he doesn't tell Laban of his plans. He just leaves.

When Laban finds out, he pursues Jacob. He confronts his son-in-law, who justifies his actions by accusing Laban of treating him unfairly and changing his wages ten times. We don't know if Jacob exaggerates this to make his point or not.

Eventually the pair work through their differences, and they part peacefully.

Though it's understandable to be upset when people lie to us, do we behave with integrity in how we deal with them? How do we react when others treat us poorly?

[Read Laban's story in Genesis 24:29–51; 27:41–28:5; 29:1–29; and 30:25–31:55.]

Jacob

When Rebekah sends Jacob away, she promises to send for him when his brother's anger subsides and it's safe for him to return. She never does.

Jacob leaves with his parents' blessing and their instruction to marry one of Laban's daughters. As we learned in the chapter about Laban, Jacob does just that, times two. He marries both of Laban's daughters, Leah and Rachel. He works for his father-in-law a total of twenty years before God tells him to return home.

His trips mark two noteworthy events in his life, one when he leaves home and the other when he returns.

First, when Jacob leaves home to go to Uncle Laban, he stops for the night along the way. He takes a stone and uses it for a pillow. It must have worked because soon he's asleep. That night he has a dream. He sees a stairway stretching between earth and heaven.

Angels travel the stairway and God stands at the top. He says, "I'm the Lord, the God of your grandfather Abraham and your father Isaac. I'll give this land to you and your descendants, making them too numerous to count. Through you and your offspring, all people will be blessed. And I'll be with you wherever you go and bring you back safely to this place."

When Jacob awakes, he takes his stone pillow, tips it upright, and pours oil on it. He pledges to serve God if the Lord will do what he promised.

This is Jacob's first recorded interaction with the Almighty, but it won't be his last.

Now full of confidence, he continues his journey. God blesses his time with Laban, giving him a family and flocks.

Twenty years later, Jacob returns home. Since his mother never sent word it was safe to come back, he has every reason to suspect Esau still intends to kill him.

Yet God says to go, and Jacob goes.

After his parting clash with Laban, Jacob plans for his confrontation with Esau. Then he prays, reminding the Lord of the promise of prosperity made twenty years ago. He asks God to protect him from his brother.

Sending everyone on ahead, Jacob remains alone. That night, a man wrestles with him. Jacob can't prevail, but neither can the man. At dawn, the man touches Jacob's hip and dislocates it. But Jacob refuses to let the man go until he gives him a blessing.

The man's response is cryptic. "I'm changing your name to Israel, for you have struggled with both God and people and have overcome."

Though the Bible doesn't say if this "man" is actually a person, an angel, or some other supernatural manifestation, Jacob believes his nighttime visitor is none other than God, for he says, "I've seen God face to face and am still alive."

Jacob meets Esau, and he's no longer holding a grudge or intent on killing his brother. The two have a peaceful reunion. God holds true to his promise from twenty years prior that he would protect Jacob, and the Lord answers Jacob's prayer for safety.

These two events stand as cornerstones in Jacob's life, with God supernaturally marking his departure and his return. This prepares Jacob for what is next.

What cornerstones has God given to us? Can we see how he has prepared us for what lies ahead?

[Read Jacob's story throughout Genesis 27–35, 42, and 46–49. Discover more in Luke 1:29–33.]

Rachel

In the Bible, Rachel's story starts when Jacob's parents send him to find a wife from his mother's family. When Jacob sees Rachel, he cries and kisses her. She's beautiful, and he falls in love.

Though they marry, her dad first pawns off her older sister, Leah, on Jacob. The sisters become co-wives, forever vying for their husband's affections. Rachel, however, remains Jacob's favorite wife.

Though Jacob loves Rachel more than Leah, it's Leah who has children, while Rachel spends years struggling with infertility. Rachel becomes jealous of her sister. Morality aside, this is a practical reason not to have multiple wives, especially ones who are also sisters.

In desperation, Rachel offers her maidservant to Jacob to produce children in her place. Jacob should have known better than to accept this, especially seeing how badly it worked out for his grandmother, Sarah, when she gave Hagar to Abraham to produce a child.

He also should have remembered his father-in-law's parting words to him, with Laban's stern warning to not marry any other women. Though Scripture never says Jacob married Rachel's maid-servant, his actions still go against the intent of his father-in-law's wishes.

But there's more.

Later, in a move reminiscent of Esau trading his birthright to Jacob for food, Rachel trades Leah a night with her husband for some mandrakes. (Non-biblical sources say it's a plant believed to have magical powers, possibly including fertility.) Ironically, while Rachel looks to a magical plant to get pregnant, Jacob plants a seed in Leah for another child.

God eventually answers Rachel's prayers for a son, and Joseph is born. Later, Rachel asks God for another boy. Tragically, she dies giving birth to her second son, Benjamin.

Though she is a beautiful woman with a loving husband, Rachel's life is filled with conflict and in wanting what she doesn't have.

Are we happy with what God gives us or do we desire more? When God doesn't provide what we want, when we want it, do we make poor choices to receive it on our own?

[Read Rachel's story in Genesis 29–31 and 35:16–20. Discover more in Ruth 4:11.]

Leah

While Rachel is most attractive, her older sister, Leah, isn't. Jacob wants to marry Rachel, not Leah. But Rachel's father pawns off Leah on Jacob instead. When Jacob protests, he's given Rachel too. Suddenly, the two sisters go from their father's control to competing with one another for their husband's affections.

Jacob loves Rachel but not Leah—though not so much that he won't sleep with her. Because Jacob doesn't love her, God sympathizes with her situation and blesses her with children. First there's Reuben, then Simeon, followed by Levi and Judah.

When childless Rachel offers Jacob her handmaid to make babies in her stead, Leah does the same thing—thereby escalating the competition.

Sometime later Leah gets pregnant again and has Issachar and then Zebulun. She also gives birth to a daughter, Dinah.

After all this, Rachel has Joseph, and much later she dies giving birth to Benjamin. At last, it seems, Leah will no longer need to compete with her sister for Jacob's attention. But the reminder of Rachel forever looms, with Jacob showing favoritism to Rachel's sons, Joseph and Benjamin, over Leah's.

As a poetic footnote to Leah's story, we read that Jacob later asks his family to bury him next to Leah in the family plot. Rachel lies buried alone in another place.

Leah's father gives her in marriage to a man who doesn't want her, but God cares for her, blessing her with many children and a long life.

Whether we're loved or unloved in this world, do we know that God's love for us is unconditional and surpasses what anyone else could offer? When we find ourselves in a competition, how can we best respond in a God-honoring way?

[Read Leah's story in Genesis 29:15–30:21 and 49:29–31. Discover more in Ruth 4:11.]

Bilhah

Bilhah and Zilpah aren't familiar names in the Bible, yet their contribution to the nation of Israel is significant.

When Laban's two daughters marry Jacob, their father gives them each a wedding gift: a servant. To his daughter Leah, he gives his servant Zilpah, while to his daughter Rachel, he gives Bilhah. These two servants shouldn't have had a significant role in the Bible, but that's not how their story unfolds. Their lives have a distressing parallel to Hagar who preceded them.

Here's Bilhah's story:

In her desperation to have children, childless Rachel offers her servant, Bilhah, to Jacob to make babies in her place. Her foolish husband agrees, impregnating his wife's servant—twice. As a result, she gives birth to Dan and Naphtali.

In a sad sidenote, Bilhah's stepson Reuben later sleeps with her. Though aware of what happened, Jacob (Israel) does nothing about it. This suggests that both Jacob and Reuben view Bilhah as property more than a person. This isn't God's perspective but man's perversion, which resulted from sin.

Throughout all this, Bilhah has no say in what happens to her. As a servant, she must obey her mistress. And she's a voiceless victim to her stepson's lust.

But as God often does, he watches out for the underdog, with Bilhah's offspring becoming part of his chosen people. This means that of Jacob's twelve sons, two come from Bilhah, with two of the tribes of Israel descending from her.

Regardless of what happens to us, do we believe God is on our side? How should we respond when people use us as objects and don't treat us as they should?

[Read Bilhah's story in Genesis 30:1–8 and 35:22.]

Zilpah

As we covered in the previous chapter, Bilhah and Zilpah are wedding gifts to Laban's daughters Rachel and Leah.

When childless Rachel, frustrated over Leah's fruitfulness, gives her servant Bilhah to Jacob to produce children, Leah responds by doing the same thing, offering her servant, Zilpah, to sleep with Jacob. Just like Bilhah, Zilpah gets pregnant twice. She gives birth to Gad and Asher.

As a result, these two servants—Bilhah and Zilpah—produce four sons for Jacob. Even though they're not from his two wives, these four sons are included in the twelve boys who eventually become the twelve tribes of Israel.

Zilpah and Bilhah have nothing to say in what happens to them, but their offspring comprise four of Israel's twelve tribes, or one third of the nation.

What should we do when we find ourselves in a situation we have no control over? When others treat us badly, do we maintain our trust in God anyway?

[Read Zilpah's story in Genesis 30:9–13.]

Reuben

Reuben is the oldest son of Jacob and Leah. We learn more about him through three stories from his life. Each one could stem from the fact that he is the eldest brother.

First, in an account that reveals his negative side, Reuben sleeps with his father's concubine Bilhah. His actions are even more distasteful—as if it were possible—when we consider that Bilhah is also the mother of two of his half-brothers and effectively his stepmom.

We earlier noted that Jacob treated Bilhah as property more than a person. Reuben's attitude toward her mirrors his father's perspective. As the first-born son, he may have a sense of entitlement to what belongs to his parents. This certainly doesn't justify what he did, but it might explain his mindset. Though Jacob knows what his son did, he takes no action to correct Reuben or protect Bilhah.

Later, we witness another side of Reuben, when he attempts to do what is right and rescue his younger brother Joseph from the hands of their jealous brothers. His brothers want to kill him, but Reuben talks them out of it. His plan is to later rescue Joseph and free him, but this doesn't happen because the brothers sell Joseph to slave traders when Reuben isn't around.

Years later, after Joseph's brothers learn he is still alive, Reuben takes responsibility with his father to guarantee the safe return of his youngest brother Benjamin. We don't know if his motivation is to appease his guilt from failing to prevent his brothers from selling Joseph into slavery, or if he's accepting responsibility as the oldest son to take the lead in resolving a tough situation. It could be a bit of both.

But the important thing is, in these last two examples, Reuben strives to do what is right.

If our past haunts us, do we let it define us or does it motivate us to do better? Jesus forgives our sins, but have we made mistakes we refuse to forgive ourselves for?

[Read Reuben's story in Genesis 29:32; 30:14–16; 35:22; 37:21–30; 42:18–37; and 49:3–4.]

Simeon (1)

Simeon is the second oldest son of Jacob and Leah. The Bible shares two stories about Simeon. The first concerns him and his brother Levi, which we'll cover in the next chapter.

The other story relates to his brother Joseph and occurs about two decades after Joseph's brothers sell him as a slave. Through multiple trials, Joseph has conducted himself well and risen to a place of power in Egypt, where he oversees the distribution of grain during a prolonged famine. Joseph's brothers (minus their youngest brother, Benjamin) go to Egypt to buy grain, so their family won't starve.

Joseph recognizes his brothers, but they don't recognize him. He treats them harshly. This isn't to pay them back for the wrong they did to him, but to test their character. He wants to see if his brothers have changed.

He accuses them of being spies and throws them all in prison for three days. Then he releases nine of them and sends them home with food. But he keeps Simeon locked up.

He warns them sternly to not return without their youngest brother, Benjamin. Though he knows who they are, he claims this is to prove they haven't lied to him and to show they aren't spies. Until they do this, he will not sell them any more grain and Simeon will remain in jail.

The nine brothers return home and tell Jacob what happened. He forbids them to return with Benjamin and secure Simeon's release. Jacob considers Simeon as dead and prohibits Benjamin from going.

When the food they bought is gone, Jacob tells his boys to return to get more. They remind him that they can't unless they return with Benjamin. At last, he relents, and Benjamin joins his nine brothers to go to Egypt to buy food and secure Simeon's release.

When they reach Egypt, Joseph frees Simeon. We'll pick up the conclusion of the story in the chapter about Joseph. Until then, let's consider Simeon's situation.

The Bible doesn't say why Joseph picked Simeon to remain locked up while his brothers go free. It may have been random, it may have been strategic, or it may have been because Simeon and Joseph's relationship was the most strained among the brothers.

We don't know why, but we do know that Simeon languished in prison while his brothers went home to their families, eating the food they had bought and making no effort to return to secure his release. In responding to his father, Judah notes they could've gone to Egypt and returned twice had they not delayed.

Simeon is no doubt counting the days until they come back to rescue him. He knows how long the journey will take. He knows when they should return. That day comes and goes, but he's still in jail. He continues counting. At twice the number of days, he's still there. Surely, he assumes his family has abandoned him to suffer in prison until he dies.

How happy he must've been—although a bit peeved at how long it took—when he's released from jail and reunited with his brothers.

How do we respond when something takes twice as long as we think it should? Do we trust God to be faithful to us even if our family or friends let us down?

[Read Simeon's story in Genesis 29:33; 42:21–36; 43:23; and 49:5–7.]

Levi (1)

Levi is the third son of Jacob and Leah. Scripture shares only one story about Levi, an account of something he and his brother Simeon do. Their younger sister Dinah, who we'll cover in a few chapters, is raped by Shechem, who then wants to marry her.

When Jacob hears of this, he does nothing, for his sons are out in the fields. However, when news of the tragedy reaches the boys, they rush home and pretend to go along with Shechem's request to wed their sister.

But they insist he undergo circumcision first, along with everyone in the city. The men agree, assuming this will allow them to intermarry with Jacob's family and acquire all their livestock and property.

As the men in town recover from their circumcisions, Levi and Simeon attack them, slaughtering every man to avenge their sister's defilement. Then the other brothers loot the town and carry off the wealth, women, and children.

Although Jacob criticizes Simeon and Levi for their excessive reaction—and the subsequent risk to the entire family should neighboring towns take revenge—the brothers feel justified in avenging their sister's dishonor, despite the risk of retaliation.

Dinah's rape is a serious assault which deserves punishment, but killing the perpetrator and all the men who live in the city is an excessive response, one that far outweighs the crime.

Several centuries later, when Moses gives the people the Law, he says retribution should be an eye for an eye (Exodus 21:23–25). This command is not an encouragement to seek revenge, but a call to avoid excessive retaliation. It's a directive of moderation.

Clearly Levi and Simeon's response to Dinah's rape was excessive and uncalled for. But they didn't have God's Law to guide them; they only had their own sense of justice.

Still, Jacob remembers what his two sons did, and on his deathbed he criticizes the violence they committed. So should we.

Yet despite what Levi did, God sets apart his descendants to serve him in the temple. From among his clan, Aaron and his offspring will serve as priests.

How do we respond when we encounter injustice? Do we react at all, or do we overreach with an excessive response?

[Read Levi's story in Genesis 29:34; 34:24–31; and 49:5–7. Discover more in Numbers 26:59.]

Judah

Judah is the fourth of Jacob's sons. His mother is Leah. Judah has three boys: Er, Onan, and Shelah. When Er is old enough, Judah finds a wife for him named Tamar (1).

Er is a wicked man, however, and God kills him. Judah then gives Tamar to his second son, Onan, to produce children with her in his dead brother's stead. Onan doesn't cooperate, however, and God kills him too.

Though the custom is to pass Tamar on to Shelah, Judah doesn't. Instead, he sends her home to live with her parents as a widow until Shelah is older. But this is a ruse.

When Tamar realizes Judah lied to her and has no intention of following through with his promise, she takes drastic action. She covers her face to disguise herself as a prostitute. Not knowing who she is, Judah propositions her, leaving his seal, cord, and staff with her as pledge for future payment. But later his representative can't find her to pay her what Judah promised or retrieve his pledges for compensation.

He sets the whole matter aside. But this doesn't mean it's over.

Three months later he learns his daughter-in-law is pregnant due to an act of prostitution. Judah proclaims judgment on her: execution by stoning for her sin.

In response, she produces his seal, cord, and staff and says the owner of these items is the father. Judah confesses his guilt and declares her as more righteous than he. He doesn't sleep with her again.

Judah does Tamar wrong, first for promising his third son to her and not following through, then for using her as a prostitute, and last for condemning her to die.

When have we made promises we had no intention of keeping? When our sins are exposed, are we quick to admit our guilt?

[Read Judah's story in Genesis 29:35; 37:26–27; 38:1–26; 43:1–10; and 49:8–12. Discover more in Matthew 1:2–3.]

Tamar (1)

Tamar is a victim who takes extreme action to vindicate herself. She's the daughter-in-law of Judah, suffers at his hand, responds with guile, and gets pregnant through him. Talk about a messed-up situation.

We've shared most of her story in the chapter on Judah. There we acknowledged that what Judah did was wrong, but that doesn't mean Tamar is innocent of wrongdoing.

She could have been content to live with her parents as a widow, but she's not. She goes to extreme measures to avenge herself of Judah's mistreatment. To do so, she poses as a prostitute and sleeps with her father-in-law. He impregnates her. As a result, Tamar gives birth to twins: Perez and Zerah.

Judah, Tamar, and Perez are all ancestors of Jesus, and Matthew lists Tamar in Jesus's genealogy. She's one of only four women so honored.

Do two wrongs make a right? When we're victimized, do we respond with God-honoring integrity?

[Read Tamar's story in Genesis 38:6–26. Discover more in Ruth 4:12 and Matthew 1:1–3.]

Dan

Dan is Jacob's fifth son. His mother is Bilhah, Rachel's servant, who serves as a surrogate mother for her mistress.

When Dan is born, it's not Jacob who names him, or even Bilhah. Rachel gives the boy his name. She says he's proof that God has vindicated her barren condition, having heard her prayers and given her a son—albeit through Bilhah.

The Bible doesn't tell us any more about Dan, but as one of Jacob's (Israel's) twelve sons, one of the twelve tribes of Israel comes from Dan and his line.

How do we respond when someone takes credit for something we did, like Rachel claiming Bilhah's son as her own? If our life seems to go without notice, do we realize we still matter to God?

[Read Dan's story in Genesis 30:6 and 49:16–17.]

Naphtali

Jacob's sixth son is the second child of Bilhah. Again, just as with his brother Dan, Rachel names Bilhah's boy. She calls him Naphtali.

Rachel's explanation reveals the depth of her motivation. She says she's had a great struggle with her sister, and Naphtali's birth proves she has won. This means Naphtali's conception and birth occur merely so Rachel can one-up her older sister. This stands as a misguided reason to have a baby.

Although the Bible doesn't tell us much about Dan, it mentions even less about Naphtali. Even so, he's one of Jacob's sons, and his descendants become one of the twelve tribes of Israel (Jacob).

Regardless of the circumstances of our birth, are we doing all we can with the life God has given us? If the structure of our family is a bit unusual, how do we treat them?

[Read Naphtali's story in Genesis 30:8 and 49:21.]

Gad (1)

As we've already covered, after Naphtali is born Rachel proclaims that his birth gives her victory over her sister, Leah.

Leah, however, doesn't accept this without a fight. She stoops to her sister's tactics and has Jacob sleep with her handmaid, Zilpah. As a result of this ill-advised union, Gad enters the world. He is Jacob's seventh son and Zilpah's first child.

If things weren't confusing enough already, Gad's arrival makes it even more so. He has six brothers, all half-brothers. Four are from his mother's mistress, Leah. And two are from his mother's counterpart, Bilhah, who is Rachel's servant. This makes one dad, three moms, and seven boys. In case you don't already know, it's going to get even more convoluted.

As with Dan and Naphtali, the birth mother doesn't get to name her son. Being the surrogate child bearer, Zilpah has no say in the matter. Instead, her mistress, Leah, names him, proclaiming her good fortune for his birth. To Leah, Gad represents a competition, with his arrival allowing her to outdo her sister in their misguided rivalry.

The Bible tells us nothing more about Gad. It's easy to dismiss him as a product of two sisters trying to upstage each other. Yet God recognizes his value. Gad takes his place among Jacob's other sons and his offspring become a tribe of Israel.

How do we react when people dismiss us? Do we think God values us regardless of what other people say or do?

[Read Gad's story in Genesis 30:11 and 49:19.]

Asher

Leah, having four sons of her own and a fifth through her maidservant, Zilpah, isn't satisfied by claiming five sons to her sister's one (who came through Rachel's maidservant).

Leah again gives Zilpah to Jacob to sleep with. Zilpah conceives and gives birth to her second son. Leah says his birth makes her happy. This totals eight boys for Jacob so far.

Like the other three surrogate sons (Dan, Naphtali, and Gad), Scripture tells us little more about Asher, except for one indirect mention in the New Testament.

After Jesus is born, his parents take him to the temple when he is eight days old. There they meet a prophetess named Anna. An eighty-four-year-old widow, Anna spends much of her time in the temple worshiping, fasting, and praying. She approaches Joseph, Mary, and baby Jesus, giving thanks to God for this child who will fulfill the words of the prophets.

Why do we mention Anna in the story about Asher? She's his descendant, a member of his tribe.

It's only an estimate, but Anna comes about forty generations after Asher.

This serves as a reminder that we don't know what our future generations may do. They may take noteworthy, God-honoring actions. Or they may not do so well.

Though we can't directly influence what our unknown offspring may or may not do, we can pray for future generations, even though we'll be gone before they arrive. This is hard to do, but it is possible.

More tangibly, we can point our family in the right direction by doing all we can to raise them well, so that they might one day put their faith in Jesus and serve him.

The rest, we'll leave up to God.

How well do we do at praying for our family? What about praying for the descendants who will follow us after we're gone?

[Read Asher's story in Genesis 30:13; 35:26; and 49:20. Discover more in Luke 2:36–38.]

Issachar

Issachar is Jacob's ninth son and Leah's fifth. That's all Scripture tells us about him. But we can imagine what his life might be like.

With eight older brothers—four full brothers and four half-brothers—Issachar arrives to a packed household. We can suspect he receives little attention.

It's easy to see him getting lost.

Issachar does nothing—good or bad—to record for us in Scripture. I'm not sure if we should be relieved or disappointed.

Yet he is one of Jacob's sons, and his descendants become one of Israel's twelve tribes.

How has our birth order affected the attention we receive and how we view ourselves? What should we accept about our circumstances and what should we seek to rise above?

[Read Issachar's story in Genesis 30:18; 35:23; and 46:14.]

Zebulun

After Issachar comes Zebulun. If you're keeping track, Zebulun is Jacob's tenth boy and Leah's sixth. If we speculated that Issachar received little attention in his large family, it may be even more true for young Zebulun.

However, Zebulun is Leah's last son. She may treat him as her baby, regardless of how old he becomes.

Just like his older brother, Gad, Zebulun's name does come up again in the Bible in the mention of one of his descendants. Fast forward to the book of Judges. One of the nation's judges is Elon. He comes from the tribe of Zebulun, a direct descendant of Zebulun. Elon leads the nation for a decade.

If we are the youngest or feel like the least in our family (or work or church), have we ever considered how God views us? Do we derive our value from our position in the world or from our right standing with God?

[Read Zebulun's story in Genesis 30:20; 35:23; and 49:13. Discover more in Judges 12:11–12.]

Dinah

Dinah is the only daughter of Jacob and Leah. She is born after Zebulun. Tragically, Shechem, a Hivite prince, rapes her. After his initial act of lust, he falls in love with her, offering to provide whatever her family asks in payment to transact the marriage. He demands his father make this happen.

Jacob doesn't respond to his daughter's rape. We don't know if he's too scared to deal with it or merely waiting for his sons to return.

While her father fails to act, two of Dinah's brothers, Simeon and Levi, do. They retaliate without Jacob's knowledge. After killing Shechem and all the men of the village, they liberate their sister and leave. Was this revenge, a rescue, or both?

After this we hear nothing more about Dinah. Though we know what happened to her and what happened because of her, we know nothing about what she said, did, or thought.

Did she appreciate her brothers for rescuing her? Was she happy they killed Shechem? Or did she have a different outlook? Despite the horrific start to their relationship, could she have accepted being Shechem's wife—or even embraced it? Might she have mourned the death of her new husband?

Though not causing it or asking for it to happen, how might she have felt knowing her brothers massacred all the men of an entire town on her behalf?

How do we respond when others mistreat us? How do we react when others decide our fate without asking our opinion?

[Read Dinah's story in Genesis 30:21 and 34:1–29.]

Joseph (1)

We've already encountered a bit about Joseph in previous chapters. Joseph is Jacob's eleventh son and Rachel's first. Since Rachel is Jacob's favorite wife, it shouldn't surprise us that her firstborn, Joseph, becomes Jacob's favorite son.

Jacob gives Joseph a brightly-colored coat, which sets him apart from his brothers. He has a dream about his family bowing down to him, which irritates his brothers even more.

Later, Jacob sends Joseph out to check up on his older brothers as they tend to the flocks. They decide to kill him, but Reuben talks them out of it. They throw Joseph into a pit instead, and Reuben secretly plans to rescue him. But before he can, the other brothers sell Joseph as a slave to make some extra money.

Then they fabricate evidence to suggest that wild animals killed Joseph. Jacob mourns the apparent death of his favorite son, and his brothers forget about him—for the most part.

Fast-forward two decades, and we see Joseph's brothers bowing before a ruler in Egypt as they seek to buy grain so they won't starve. They don't know they're bowing before Joseph, just like his dream foresaw. Eventually he reveals himself to them and they reconcile. Then Joseph sends for his entire family to come live in Egypt.

Between these two events in Joseph's life, however, he undergoes difficulties and suffers greatly. Here's a synopsis:

First, the slave traders sell him to Potiphar. Joseph conducts himself well, and Potiphar's household prospers under Joseph's direction. But Potiphar's wife tries to seduce Joseph. He resists but ends up in prison in spite of his integrity.

There Joseph finds favor with the warden, who puts him in charge of the other prisoners. While incarcerated, Joseph correctly interprets the dreams of two fellow prisoners. As predicted, one is executed and the other freed. Joseph requests that the released prisoner ask Pharaoh to free him. The man doesn't.

But when Pharaoh has a troubling dream, the man remembers Joseph. Joseph interprets the dream and offers wise advice on how to prepare for an upcoming seven-year famine.

In the end, Pharaoh honors Joseph's wisdom by putting him in charge and gives Joseph an Egyptian wife. They have two sons, Manasseh and Ephraim. Unlike his brothers, Joseph doesn't have a tribe named after him. Instead, there are two: the tribe of Manasseh and the tribe of Ephraim.

Do we act like Joseph and hold onto our integrity even if we might face punishment? Regardless of our circumstances, do we always do our best work?

[Read Joseph's story throughout Genesis 37 and 39–50. Discover more in Exodus 13:19; Psalm 105:16–22; Acts 7:9–15; and Hebrews 11:21–22.]

Benjamin (1)

Jacob's eleven sons and daughter Dinah are all born while he works for his uncle Laban. After twenty years, God sends Jacob and his family back to Canaan. This is where Jacob's twelfth and final son, Benjamin, is born. His arrival marks a bittersweet moment, however, for Jacob's beloved wife Rachel dies during childbirth. In this one moment he gains a son and loses a wife.

This means Benjamin grows up without a mom. Though he effectively has three stepmothers, Scripture doesn't say if any of them attempt to mother him. Bilhah, as Rachel's handmaid, would be the logical choice, continuing to serve her mistress even after her death. But we don't know if she assumes this role or not. Though we can surmise that all three women care for Benjamin's physical needs, we don't know if anyone tries to fill the supportive role of mother.

Though Rachel is gone, sons Joseph and Benjamin live on, embodying her memory to their father. When Joseph's brothers sell Joseph as a slave and convince Jacob he is dead, Jacob coddles Benjamin even more, as the last living connection to Rachel's memory.

Given this, it's understandable that Jacob objects when the Egyptian ruler (later revealed as Joseph) insists the brothers bring Benjamin to Egypt. Nonetheless, Jacob eventually relents, knowing a return trip is necessary to secure the food they need to survive.

Although the Bible tells us much about the older brother, Joseph, it reveals little about the younger brother, Benjamin.

There are, however, three notable people in Scripture who are Benjamin's descendants. One is King Saul, Israel's first ruler (1 Samuel 9:1, 16). The others are Mordecai and Esther, also known as Hadassah, who becomes queen (Esther 2:5–17). We'll cover all three in upcoming chapters.

If we're the youngest or ever consider ourselves to be the least, are we willing to let God's perspective inform our self-image? What role does God want us to play in our family?

[Read Benjamin's story throughout Genesis 42–45. Discover more in Genesis 35:18 and 49:27.]

PART 3:

MOSES AND THE LAW

Jacob and his family end up in Egypt because of a famine. When the famine ends, they don't go home to the land God promised Abraham, but they stay in Egypt. There their numbers explode, and the Egyptians force them into slavery.

Four centuries later, Moses arrives and eventually leads them to freedom and back to the promised land. He also receives God's instructions for right living, which we refer to as the Law, the Law of Moses. This tells the people what to do and not to do so that they may be right with God.

After Moses, we'll continue our biblical story arc to Joshua, the judges, and the people begging for a king to lead them instead of God. But first we must cover someone else, someone you may have never heard about.

Jochebed

After the seven-year famine ends, Jacob and his family don't go home. Instead, they stay in Egypt. They prosper there and remain for four centuries. This is where we pick up our story.

In the intervening years, the Egyptians have enslaved Jacob's offspring, forcing them to do manual labor for their building projects. Fearing the mushrooming population of the Israelites, Pharaoh orders his people to throw every Hebrew baby boy into the Nile River.

One mother, however, senses something unique in her child and decides to ignore the edict. She hides her son for as long as she can. Eventually, unable to conceal him any longer, she does put him in the Nile River, but not before laying him in a watertight basket.

She strategically places the basket where a compassionate person might find it. The woman's daughter hides nearby to see what happens to her baby brother.

When Pharaoh's daughter comes to the river to bathe, she discovers the baby and wants to keep him as her own. The baby's sister steps out of hiding and offers to find a woman to nurse him; she gets her mother. Although the boy should die, Pharaoh's daughter saves him and even pays his biological mother to care for him.

Once weaned, his mother gives him back to Pharaoh's daughter, who names him Moses. This Hebrew mother's name is Jochebed and she has two other children, Aaron and Miriam.

Jochebed, like many moms, sees promise in her child and takes extraordinary measures to protect him so he can reach his potential.

Who has seen promise in us and made a difference in our lives? Who can we help reach their potential?

[Read Jochebed's story in Exodus 2:1–10. Discover more in Numbers 26:59.]

Moses

Moses receives more coverage in the Old Testament than any other character, except for King David. Abraham comes in third.

Though we could compose an entire book about Moses—and others have—let's consider five defining moments in his life. We can use these to inspire and challenge us.

For our first story, let's look at Moses being raised in the palace. He senses his calling from the Lord to lead the people and goes out to visit them. There he encounters an Egyptian mistreating one of God's people. Moses kills the Egyptian and hides the body. When he learns his homicidal act is known, he takes off to build a new life away from Egypt and his people.

Next, Moses marries and cares for his father-in-law's flocks. While out in the wilderness doing his job, Moses spots a bush ablaze in the distance that does not burn up. He investigates. There he encounters God, who sends Moses back to Egypt to rescue his people. After debating a bit with the Almighty, Moses obeys.

Third, after a series of plagues sent by God and corresponding confrontations with Pharaoh, Moses leads the people out of Egypt. In one of the Bible's best-known stories, God parts the waters of the Red Sea, and Moses leads his people to safety on the other side. When the Egyptian army gives chase, the waters crash down upon them, and they drown. Though God orchestrates this miracle, it occurs through Moses and is a result of his faith and obedience.

Another well-known story occurs when Moses is on a mountain communing with God where he receives instructions—the Ten Commandments and the Law. This at last gives the people God's rules for right living and proper conduct.

Though they may have had some inborn idea of right and wrong all along, now they understand for sure what God expects of them. They know that murder is wrong. They know that marrying a half-sister is wrong. And they know that worshiping anything other than God is wrong.

It takes time for God to give Moses his rules, and the people grow impatient. Aaron acts. He fashions an idol made from gold—a golden calf—and institutes a raucous worship celebration of the statue.

God is furious at the people and wants to wipe them out. He promises to start over and make a new nation, not of Abraham's seed, but from Moses's. Instead of accepting God's plan to make him into a great nation, Moses intercedes for the rebellious people. God hears his plea and relents. The people live because of Moses.

Last, aside from committing homicide much earlier in his life, Moses later mars his otherwise exemplary leadership by a single act of disobedience. The people are thirsty and clamor for water. God tells Moses to go to a rock and speak to it. Then water will flow forth.

Though Moses does go to the rock, he hits it twice with his staff. And instead of speaking the words God gave him, Moses utters his own. By doing so, he dishonors the Lord. Because of this single sin God won't let Moses enter the promised land.

This is a poignant reminder that if we try to approach God by following a bunch of rules—such as the Law he gave to Moses and the people—even one failure, in one area, is sufficient to disqualify us from our heavenly reward.

Fortunately, Jesus came to show us another way, something anyone can do. It's simple. All we need to do is put our faith in him (Ephesians 2:8–9).

What examples from Moses's life should we aspire to? How can we have a close, intimate relationship with God just like Moses?

[Read Moses's story throughout Exodus, Leviticus, Numbers, and Deuteronomy. Discover more in John 3:14; Acts 7:20–44; 2 Corinthians 3:7–13; and Hebrews 11:23–29.]

Aaron

A aron is the older brother of Moses. His mother is Jochebed, and his father is Amram.

God tells Aaron to go out into the wilderness to meet Moses, who is expecting him. The plan is for Aaron to serve as his brother's spokesman, because Moses doesn't think he's eloquent enough for the job God called him to do.

Aaron and Moses work together to communicate with Pharaoh and bring about the people's eventual escape from Egypt. When God gives Moses the Law, Aaron and his sons will play a vital role in leading the people in worship. In doing so, Aaron becomes the first priest, and his sons—at least the two obedient ones—continue the work, as will their descendants.

Aaron does all God asks of him, supports his younger brother Moses, and serves well as God's first priest. Despite all this exemplary behavior, however, Aaron has two blemishes in his otherwise spotless record.

Before God institutes Aaron as his priest, Aaron attempts to assume this responsibility himself. As we already learned in the chapter about Moses, it's Aaron who constructs the golden calf idol and leads the people to worship it. This isn't what God intended.

The other incident occurs later.

Aaron and Miriam criticize Moses for his choice of a wife. They also attempt to elevate themselves as spokespeople for God, since the Almighty also talks to them and not just Moses.

God hears their murmuring and isn't pleased. He burns with anger toward them for opposing Moses and seeking to promote themselves.

The Almighty strikes Miriam with leprosy, and Aaron panics. He begs Moses for forgiveness. The fact he doesn't go directly to God suggests he doesn't have as close of a relationship with the Almighty as he and Miriam thought.

Aaron escapes punishment, perhaps because he so quickly sought forgiveness.

When we sin are we quick to confess it and seek forgiveness? Have we ever attempted to elevate ourselves beyond what God has called us to do?

[Read Aaron's story in Exodus 4–12 and 16–19. Discover more in Deuteronomy 10:6 and Luke 1:5.]

Miriam (1)

Miriam is the older sister of Moses and the sister of Aaron. Recall that young Miriam watches at a distance to see what happens after her mom places baby Moses in a basket in the Nile River. In this we see an obedient and brave girl.

Later, as an adult, Miriam becomes both a prophet and a worship leader. She directs the Israelite women in song and dance to celebrate God's rescue after they cross the sea to escape the pursuing Egyptian army.

Unfortunately, what we know best about Miriam is when she and Aaron oppose Moses out of jealousy, criticizing his choice for a wife. God's judgment is quick, instantly afflicting her with leprosy, a contagious skin disease, which was untreatable at the time.

Though Aaron is also at fault, he doesn't get leprosy. This suggests that Miriam led their tiny rebellion. Aaron sees what happened and admits his bad attitude, begging Moses to intervene. Moses does, and God implicitly heals Miriam.

A few years later Miriam dies. There's no mention of the people mourning her death. This is a sad end to a once-promising life. Though Miriam starts well as a brave and obedient daughter and later becomes a prophet and worship leader, she lets jealousy define her later life. God is not pleased.

What can we do to finish strong? When we falter, how do we react when confronted with our shortcomings?

[Read Miriam's story in Exodus 2:1–10; Exodus 15:20–21; Numbers 12:1–15; and Numbers 20:1.]

Caleb (1)

After the Hebrew people escape Egypt, they make their way across the desert, approaching the land God promised to Abraham. Moses selects a representative from each tribe of Israel to spy out the land.

Caleb, son of Jephunneh, is one of the twelve men selected, representing the tribe of Judah. The twelve head out to discover what the land is like and do some reconnaissance so they can form a battle plan to conquer it. They spend forty days making a comprehensive tour of the area.

The group returns and presents their findings to Moses. "It's a wonderful land," they say, "but the people who live there are powerful and reside in fortified cities."

Caleb, however, offers an opposite perspective. His is the minority report. "We should leave at once and conquer the land. We can certainly do that."

But the majority disagree with Caleb. The Israelites—whose only skill is slave labor—seem no match for the inhabitants of the land. "Those people are stronger and bigger than we are," they say.

In the end, the people disregard what Caleb said and believe the majority report. They cry, grumble, and want to return to Egypt.

But Caleb—along with Joshua, one of the other spies—encourages the people to move forward under God's power to take the land.

In response, the people threaten to stone them.

Are we willing to stand up and speak God's truth even if we are a small minority? When we see others deciding to do what we believe is wrong, how do we respond?

[Read Caleb's story in Numbers 13–14. Discover more in Joshua 15:13–19 and Judges 1:12–20.]

Joshua (1)

Joshua son of Nun serves Moses, first as an aide and later as his protégé, before he eventually succeeds him. Joshua is first known as Hoshea, but Moses gives him the name of Joshua. Though there's much to examine in Joshua's life, let's focus on a few significant moments.

The young apprentice witnesses his mentor's example and is often present when Moses interacts with God. What an amazing experience this must have been. It shouldn't surprise us that Moses selects Joshua as one of the twelve men chosen to spy out the land in preparation for conquering it.

What seems strange is Joshua's silence when Caleb gives his recommendation to go at once to take the land. Caleb seems to stand alone against the other spies who cower in fear.

Joshua, however, later joins Caleb to counter the majority report as the pair try to convince the people to move forward in faith, under God's power. They continue their efforts, until the people threaten to kill them.

About forty years later, when Moses dies, Joshua succeeds him. He successfully leads the people to conquer the promised land. Though an entire generation has died in the desert because of their grumbling and lack of faith, Joshua and Caleb are still alive. Joshua rewards Caleb's faithfulness by assigning him a portion of the land the people conquered.

Joshua dies at 110 years old. Although Moses wisely appointed Joshua as his successor, Joshua fails to follow his mentor's example. He dies without having groomed anyone to replace him.

When we fail to speak up when we should, what can we do to correct our error? What are we doing to ensure that what we have started can continue when we're gone?

[Read Joshua's story in Exodus 17:9–14 and Numbers 13–14, as well as the entire book of Joshua. Discover more in Numbers 11:28; 27:18–23; Deuteronomy 3:21–28; and Deuteronomy 31.]

Balak

Because of the people's lack of faith, God turns them away from the promised land. They spend forty years in the desert, one year for each day the spies were on their mission. We resume our story four decades later as they finally prepare to conquer the nations before them under the leadership of Moses and then Joshua.

Balak son of Zippor, king of Moab, sees the approaching Hebrew people and fears they will attack his land. Believing he cannot prevail with military force alone, he sends for Balaam, a practitioner of divination, to curse the encroaching horde.

Balaam refuses, but Balak persists. When Balaam agrees to appear before Balak, he repeatedly reminds the king and his emissaries that he can only say what the Lord puts in his mouth.

Balak accepts this condition. He sacrifices seven bulls and seven rams as Balaam instructs. Then, prompted by God, Balaam blesses the Hebrew people.

Frustrated that Balaam didn't dispense curses as requested, the desperate Balak asks Balaam to try again. The outcome is the same.

Having not learned his lesson, Balak begs Balaam a third time to spew forth curses against the danger that threatens Moab. Once again, Balaam speaks blessings instead of curses.

Balak is furious with Balaam. Yet it's his own fault. Balaam declined to come to Balak in the first place and warned he could only say what God told him to say.

But Balak was too afraid and pushed forward when he shouldn't have. His ill-advised actions in seeking to curse his enemies had the opposite effect.

When has our fear caused us to do the wrong thing? When have we failed to see God at work and persisted to pursue our own path?

[Read Balak's story in Numbers 22–24. Discover more in Micah 6:5 and Revelation 2:14.]

Balaam

Balaam son of Beor practices divination. His work must be of some renown, for when Balak seeks a supernatural edge over the approaching Hebrew people, he sends for Balaam to proclaim curses against the Israelites.

God tells Balaam not to go and he doesn't. We affirm him for doing what God said.

But Balak persists and sends a second delegation to fetch Balaam. The seer again seeks a word from God about what to do, even though the Almighty had already made his position clear. This time God says to go but for Balaam to watch what he says, speaking only the words God gives him to say.

At each step of the story Balaam does exactly what God tells him to do. We can applaud him for his obedience.

Yet not so fast.

In the end, God isn't pleased with Balaam. We're left to wonder why, for it seems Balaam obeyed God flawlessly and did everything as instructed.

But the hint for God's displeasure comes from what Balaam did after the second emissary delegation arrived. Though God had already made it clear Balaam wasn't to go, the greedy seer asked a second time. Instead of repeating his prior instruction, God relented and allowed Balaam to go.

Though this is what the prophet desired to do all along, it wasn't what God wanted. The rest of Scripture confirms God's displeasure with Balaam.

When we don't like what God tells us to do, do we keep asking anyway? Might there have ever been a time when we thought we were being obedient, yet our attitude displeased God?

[Read Balaam's story in Numbers 22–24. Discover more in Numbers 31:8; 2 Peter 2:15–16; Jude 1:11; and Revelation 2:14.]

Rahab

The Hebrew people's first opportunity to take the promised land didn't work out. Forty years after this first failure, Joshua—who is now in charge—sends out two spies instead of twelve.

As the two spies explore Jericho, they stay with Rahab, a prostitute. We don't know if they seek her for her services or merely for a place to hide from public view.

Learning of their presence, Jericho's king commands Rahab to turn over the two men. In a treasonous act, she hides them instead. She lies to the king, saying they've already left, but that she doesn't know where they went.

Rahab realizes God favors Israel and that he will give the city to them. In exchange for protecting the spies, she asks for her family's safety. Joshua promises to spare Rahab and her family when the Israelites raze the city. After the destruction of Jericho and its inhabitants, Rahab goes to live with the Israelites.

In the New Testament, Matthew reveals Rahab as one of Jesus's direct ancestors and the great-great-grandmother of King David.

She's honored as only one of four women listed in Jesus's family tree. She's also affirmed as a person of faith, one of only two women included in the list of God's most faithful followers in Hebrews 11.

Finally, James confirms Rahab is righteous because of her courageous actions in protecting the two spies.

While our reaction may be to judge Rahab for her profession, God sees her differently, as a woman of faith. He rewards her accordingly. He doesn't judge her by her work, but he does affirm her for her faith.

When have we judged someone because of their job or reputation? How can we better appreciate the people God affirms?

[Read Rahab's story in Joshua 2:1–21 and 6:17–25. Discover more in Matthew 1:1–5; Hebrews 11:31; and James 2:25.]

Deborah (2)

As we covered in the chapter on Joshua, he dies without naming a successor. A lack of leadership makes it hard for the people to keep their focus on God, and they languish as a nation. The book of Judges summarizes this succinctly: it is a time when Israel has no king, and everyone does whatever they want (Judges 21:25).

During this time, they encounter repeated cycles of disobedience, oppression, rescue, and obedience—only to fall back into ignoring God. The rescue portion of each cycle comes from a judge. This is not someone who decides legal cases. Instead, these judges are leaders, often military ones.

Three of these judges are Gideon, Samson, and Deborah. Let's start by looking at Deborah.

Though called a judge, Deborah is primarily a prophetess, a person who hears from God and proclaims his words to others. She is the only female judge in the book of Judges. And unlike the other judges listed, she's the only one to hold court.

Aligned with her primary calling, Deborah receives a prophetic message for Barak. Through her,

God commands him to raise an army and attack their enemy. God even promises that Barak will prevail, but the fearful man declines.

Barak refuses to do what God tells him to do unless Deborah goes with him. She consents but prophesies that because of his reluctance, the honor of killing the enemy's leader, Sisera, will go to a woman.

Deborah lives in a male-dominated society. Yet, when a man doesn't do what he's supposed to, she steps forward and acts. We commend her for her faith and her bravery.

When others won't do what they're supposed to do for God, are we willing to step in to help make it happen? Are we sometimes like Barak, lacking the courage to do what God tells us to do?

[Read Deborah's story in Judges 4–5.]

Barak

God gives the prophetess Deborah a message for Barak. God wants him to raise a troop of 10,000 and confront the better-equipped army led by Sisera. God promises to give Barak the victory. But Barak balks.

Barak is the son of Abinoam. He lives in Kedesh in the territory of Naphtali in Israel. That's all we know about him. Though he might be a trained warrior or military leader, his reaction to God's call suggests he's anything but. His skills may reside in growing crops or raising animals, not commanding an army and defeating the enemy.

Given this assumption, his reluctance seems warranted. A farmer can't lead an army and prevail against a stronger foe—at least not from a human standpoint. But with God, all things are possible. God even promises victory.

Still, Barak is unwilling to obey—unless Deborah goes with him. As you may recall in the chapter on Aaron, Moses did the same thing when God called him. And God sent him Aaron to help.

With Deborah at his side, Barak finally obeys. Their army prevails, just as God promised. Then Deborah and Barak sing a song of praise to God.

In this story, we see Deborah as brave, while Barak comes across as a coward. Yet the book of Hebrews affirms Barak for his faith and doesn't list Deborah.

Though we may perceive Barak as a man who lacks courage, God sees him as a man of noteworthy faith.

How do we react when God calls us to do something we feel unqualified to do? Do we let our faith override logic or allow logic to control us?

[Read Barak's story in Judges 4–5. Discover more in Hebrews 11:32–34.]

Jael

Deborah prophesied that the credit for killing the enemy commander, Sisera, would go to a woman. We may assume Deborah is that woman. She's not.

When Barak and Deborah lead the Israelite army and rout Sisera's forces, the enemy commander escapes. He takes refuge with a woman named Jael because her family has a connection with his country.

Jael offers him sanctuary, gives him something to drink, and stands guard at the tent opening so he can rest. Her protection is a ruse. Once he falls asleep, she drives a tent peg through his temple. Though gruesome, it may be the only means she has to kill him. She's brave enough to act and strong enough to pierce his skull.

This fulfills Deborah's prophecy.

As a tribute to Jael's valor, Deborah and Barak immortalize her actions in a song of praise.

Are the things we do worth singing about? Will future generations hear about what we do for God?

[Read Jael's story in Judges 4:17–22 and 5:24–27.]

Gideon

Gideon is an interesting judge. The Bible gives us three chapters about key events in his life. Some of what he does inspires us and provides an example to follow. Yet he does other things we should certainly avoid. But aren't we all like that, with both strengths and weaknesses?

In our first story Gideon is threshing wheat in a winepress. If this seems weird, that's because it is. But he's afraid of having his grain stolen by the Midianites, so he's working in an unlikely place where they may not notice him. Then God's angel shows up, addresses him as a mighty warrior, and tells him to go in his own strength to save his people. Gideon questions the angel, and God's emissary must prove himself to the fearful man.

After doing so, he tells Gideon to destroy his father's altar to Baal. Gideon does, but he does so at night for fear of the townspeople. When they find out what he did, they want to kill him, but his father intercedes and stops them.

We best know Gideon, however, for putting out a fleece to determine God's will. Although Gideon has already marshaled an army to attack his enemy, he asks God if he will prevail, even though the Almighty has already promised he will.

Gideon's test is simple. He'll lay a ball of wool—a fleece—on the ground. If the morning dew falls only on the wool and not the ground, Gideon will conclude he'll be victorious. The next morning the wool is dripping wet. The surrounding area is dry.

Yet Gideon doubts. He repeats the test, this time requesting the opposite outcome. The next morning, the wool is dry and the ground, wet. At this second confirmation, he believes God.

Many have followed Gideon's example of "putting out a fleece" to determine God's will. Yet we should note that God doesn't tell us to do this. Instead, the Bible merely describes what Gideon did, without commenting on the wisdom of doing so.

This story shows both Gideon's lack of confidence in God and the Almighty's patience with his doubtful servant.

Next, God tells Gideon his army of 32,000 is too big. The people will see the victory and assume they did it on their own. God desires a smaller force to prove his hand in the outcome. Whittling the army down to three hundred, Gideon moves forward in confident faith to victory, which God orchestrates.

After this, the people want to make Gideon their king. He declines, reminding them that God is their king.

Yet, after this wise response, Gideon foolishly collects a gold earring from each man's plunder. He uses this to make a golden ephod (a ceremonial garment), which the people worship instead of God.

Though Gideon at times acts with bravery, faith, and wisdom, he also doubts, tests God, and makes a foolish decision, which mark his legacy.

In what ways are we like Gideon? What lessons can we learn from his life?

[Read Gideon's story in Judges 6–8. Discover more in Hebrews 11:32–34.]

Samson

Another judge is Samson. His story begins even before his birth. An angel appears to a childless woman and tells her she'll become pregnant and have a son. The angel says the boy will be dedicated to God, even before he is born.

He then gives the woman special dietary expectations. Though we may assume these only apply while she's pregnant, the text suggests they continue after his birth. The boy, who is to be a Nazirite, also has rules to follow, such as never cutting his hair.

What a grand start to life: dedicated to God even before birth.

Yet Samson fails to live up to the Almighty's expectations for his life. He squanders his great beginning. Though God does use him to kill some of the nation's Philistine enemies, this isn't because of Samson's right behavior. Instead, God uses Samson despite his faulty character. He disrespects his parents, disobeys God, and doesn't control his sexual desires.

Samson touches a carcass, though God prohibits it. Samson also likes foreign women, also contrary to God's law. He marries a Philistine woman, but the seven-day wedding celebration doesn't go well. It's all because he challenged thirty of the men in attendance with a riddle.

They can't solve it and press his bride for the solution. She doesn't know and plies Samson for the answer. With constant tears and pleading, she wears him down and he explains it to her. She tells the thirty men, and they answer the riddle, winning the bet Samson made with them. To pay up, Samson kills thirty other men, takes their clothes, and gives them to the men at the wedding.

Then Samson abandons his new wife, and her father gives her to another. When Samson wants her back, it's too late. In retaliation, he burns their crops. The Philistines blame the woman and her father for this and kill them. Samson escalates the conflict further, slaying many more in revenge.

Another time Samson hires a prostitute.

Later he falls in love with Delilah. She proves to be his undoing.

The Philistines hire Delilah to uncover the source of Samson's strength so they can capture him and stop him from killing more of their people.

She asks him to share his secret with her and he toys with her, giving false information, but each time he edges closer to the truth. He eventually reveals that the secret to his strength is that he's never had a haircut.

She calls for the Philistines to shave his head. Then they capture him. They gouge his eyes and throw him in prison.

His hair begins to grow back, and he asks God for one final burst of strength. God grants his request, and Samson destroys the Philistine temple by taking out one of its main supports. The building crumbles, killing 3,000 Philistines and Samson along with them.

Whether little or much, have we made the most of the start we've been given in life? When we make mistakes, do we believe God can still use us?

[Read Samson's story in Judges 13–16. Discover more in Hebrews 11:32–34.]

Delilah

Delilah is infamous for her tryst with bad-boy Samson, but we know little more about her. The Bible says Samson falls in love with her, but we don't know if it's reciprocal. She may have had other reasons to pursue a relationship with him.

Whatever her initial motivation to hook up with the powerful Samson, money soon becomes a greater incentive. The Philistine leaders offer her silver if she can uncover the secret behind her lover's immense strength. She agrees.

Eager to earn her reward, she plies Samson to reveal the source of his vigor. Three times he toys with her, giving misinformation, which she accepts as truth. Each time the Philistines use this information to try to capture him. Each time they fail.

Humiliated by her inability to learn the truth, and eager to earn her payout, she badgers him. Her nagging eventually wears him down. He breaks and reveals everything to her.

Now knowing the true secret to his might, the Philistines cut his hair. Then they capture him since he now lacks the strength to escape.

Whatever Delilah thought of Samson at first, she readily sold him out for a sack of silver.

What are we willing to do to make money? Do we put wealth, power, or prestige ahead of our relationships with others—and with God?

[Read Delilah's story in Judges 16:4–21.]

Elimelek

During the time of the judges, we come across a man named Elimelek. Scripture tells us little about him, covering his story in a scant three verses.

He's married to Naomi, and they have two sons. They live in Bethlehem, which is part of Judah. There's a famine, so they head off to Moab. There Elimelek dies.

His sons both get married, one to Orpah and the other to Ruth. Then they die too.

This leaves widowed Naomi with no sons and two daughters-in-law. We'll cover them in the next few chapters.

Elimelek's life seems like a most unremarkable one. He marries, has two kids, and struggles to make a living. Then he dies.

It's depressing.

But there's more to his story. Though Elimelek dies without having done anything noteworthy in his life, he does play an essential role in Jesus's family tree. Had he not taken his family to Moab, Jesus wouldn't have been born. The following chapters, building up to Ruth, will explain.

Though we all want to make the most of our life and impact our world, we may not see the results we want. Yet our influence can continue after we're gone.

Are we making the most of our life in how we live each day? Do we believe God can use the things we do now to define the future?

[Read Elimelek's story in Ruth 1:1–3.]

Naomi

Naomi's name means *pleasant*.

Naomi, her husband, and their two boys leave their home in Judah because of a famine. They travel to Moab in search of food. While in this foreign land, Naomi's husband dies. Later, both of her married sons die too. This leaves her with two widowed daughters-in-law, Orpah and Ruth, and little hope.

Naomi blames God for her misfortune and grows resentful. She even tries to change her name to Mara, which means "bitter."

Naomi decides to return home when she hears they have food there. Orpah and Ruth head back with her, but Naomi decides this isn't fair to them. At Naomi's urging, Orpah returns to Moab to rejoin her family, but Ruth insists on staying with her mother-in-law.

Once in Juda, Naomi devises a strategy for Ruth to marry their relative, Boaz. Ruth follows her mother-in-law's instructions exactly as directed, and events play out as Naomi hopes. Boaz and Ruth soon marry. Ruth has her first child, Obed. Naomi cares for her new grandson like a son, while the local women celebrate his birth and Naomi's good fortune.

Naomi's life—like everyone's life—contains both struggle and disappointment, but God cares for her. He provides a loyal daughter-in-law and a cherished grandson, her first.

Even if life goes terribly wrong and we become bitter against God, criticizing him for our troubles, he still loves us and provides for us.

Do we trust God with our future, regardless of the situation? Have we ever blamed God for our misfortune?

[Read Naomi's story throughout Ruth 1–4.]

Orpah

Orpah is the widowed daughter-in-law of Naomi and the sister-in-law of Ruth.

When Naomi heads for home, she encourages Orpah and Ruth to stay behind. Though Ruth refuses, Orpah does the logical thing and returns.

That's the last we hear of her.

We don't know if she marries again or ever has children. We don't know how long she lives. We just know she did the sensible thing.

Orpah's sister-in-law, however, chooses the path that doesn't make sense, and God honors her for her loyalty to him and her mother-in-law.

Sometimes the sensible solution isn't the one God honors.

Who are we loyal to and why? Do we put God first even when it doesn't make sense?

[Read Orpah's story in Ruth 1:4–14.]

Ruth

Ruth is a widow. She's a foreigner; that is, she's not a Hebrew. And she remains faithful to Naomi, her mother-in-law, also a widow.

Here's Ruth's story.

When Naomi returns home to Judah from Moab, she urges Ruth to stay behind in her own country, with her own family. Ruth, however, won't consider it. She clings to her mother-in-law and pledges her allegiance to Naomi and to Naomi's God.

We can only guess at the reason behind Ruth's intense loyalty to Naomi. Having lost her husband and both sons, Naomi has become a bitter woman, so it certainly isn't her shining character that prompts Ruth's devotion.

When they return to Judah, Ruth searches for grain missed by the harvesters so that she and Naomi will have some food to eat. In doing so Ruth puts herself in a dangerous situation, should a harvester harass or take advantage of her. Yet Ruth ends up in the fields of a wealthy farmer, Boaz. He's heard of her devotion to Naomi and appreciates her hardworking nature and godly character. She finds favor with him, and he promises her protection when she's in his fields.

Naomi wants to find another husband for Ruth.

Although older, Boaz seems the ideal choice, since he's a close relative, a kinsman who can redeem her through marriage, as prescribed in the Law of Moses (Leviticus 25:25). Naomi develops a shrewd strategy for Ruth to go to Boaz at night and capture his attention. Ruth dutifully does as her mother-in-law directs. While it's unclear if Naomi's instructions cause Ruth to act in a manner considered brazen, she does gain Boaz's notice.

When Boaz and Ruth marry, the people bless her and her future children.

Ruth has her first child, a boy they name Obed. Obed is the father of Jesse, the father of David. This makes Ruth the great-grandmother of King David.

God rewards Ruth's allegiance to him and loyalty to her mother-in-law, providing Ruth with a husband, saving her from poverty, and giving her a son.

Ruth is one of four women honored by Matthew in his record of Jesus's family tree. She is his direct ancestor.

Do we have a reputation for being loyal and hardworking? Is our godly character affirmed by others?

[Read Ruth's story in Ruth 1–4. Discover more in Matthew 1:1–5.]

Boaz

Boaz is a wealthy farmer living in Judah. He was a close relative of the Elimelek we covered a few chapters ago. Boaz is also a respected man, well known for his integrity.

When Ruth goes out to glean the grain the harvesters missed, she ends up in one of Boaz's fields. He knows her by reputation, but this is the first time he sees her. Boaz approaches. He affirms her loyalty to Naomi, promises her safety in his fields, and gives her the same privileges as his laborers—even though she is but a poor widow scavenging for food.

Excited to learn that Ruth ended up in Boaz's field and favorably interacted with him, Naomi later sends Ruth to the threshing floor at night to get Boaz's attention. Ruth asks him to redeem her. In effect, she's asking him to marry her. It's a proposal of sorts.

Attracted to her, Boaz is willing, but he isn't her closest relative. Another man is. Boaz can only marry Ruth if the other man declines to do so.

Boaz immediately sets out to make Ruth his wife, deftly dealing with the other relative who could thwart his intentions.

They marry and have a baby boy. Though we don't know if Boaz has other children, this is Ruth's first.

They name him Obed. He is the grandfather of King David and a direct ancestor of Jesus.

One more thing. Remember Rahab, the prostitute who helped the spies? She's Boaz's mother.

Do people affirm us as someone with integrity? How do we treat those who are less fortunate than we are?

[Read Boaz's story in Ruth 2–4. Discover more in Matthew 1:1–5.]

~

Samuel (1)

Some time later, we encounter Samuel. Those who grew up hearing Bible stories may remember the account of young Samuel. He is the son of Elkanah and Hannah. His mother takes him to live at the temple and help Eli, the priest. Each year she visits him and gives him a little robe to wear. You may even recall a picture of the bright-eyed Samuel smiling as his mother gives him his new outfit.

This idyllic scene ignores the fact that Hannah commits Samuel to a lifetime of service before he is born; he has no say in the matter. This also requires him to leave his home to live with a stranger, a man who wasn't a good father to his own sons. How distraught young Samuel must have been over being separated from his mother and having his entire future planned for him.

Yet Samuel excels in this environment. As a young boy he can hear the voice of God, something few others can do in that day.

Though Eli is a priest, Samuel lacks the bloodline (a descendant of Aaron) to succeed him as priest. When Eli dies, however, Samuel replaces him as the leader of all Israel. The Bible also calls Samuel a prophet (a seer).

Up to this time, Israel did not have a king. God served as their king. And he used a series of judges to rescue his wayward people from their enemies and return their focus to him each time they fell away.

When Samuel grows older, he appoints his sons to take over for him. But they are corrupt, just like the sons of his mentor. Samuel must've learned his parenting skills from the inept Eli.

The elders go to Samuel and ask him to appoint a king to rule over the nation. This distresses Samuel, but the Almighty tells him it's okay. The people aren't rejecting Samuel's leadership; they're rejecting God's. Although reluctant, Samuel anoints Saul to be Israel's first king, as directed by the Lord. When Saul later falters, God tells Samuel to anoint David to replace Saul.

How do we react when we end up in a situation we didn't choose? Whether our position is grand or humble, do we serve God to the best of our abilities, like Samuel?

[Read Samuel's story in 1 Samuel 1–25. Discover more in Hebrews 11:32–34.]

PART 4:

DAVID, A MAN AFTER GOD'S OWN HEART

Though God intended to lead his people, they clamor for a king to reign over them like all the other nations. At God's direction, Samuel reluctantly gives them one. The first king is Saul. When he doesn't work out, God picks a second one, David, despite the man's shortcomings. Nevertheless, the Bible calls him a man after God's own heart (1 Samuel 13:14 and Acts 13:22).

With the kingship establishing God's people as a nation, we'll explore some of the kings and prophets who follow David. Eventually their repeated disobedience receives God's punishment, which occurs when they're conquered and deported.

But to set the stage for this, we'll first consider King Saul.

Saul (1)

Saul is the first king of Israel.

God directs Samuel, the prophet, to anoint Saul when the people ask for a human king to rule over them instead of God. Saul is a head taller than everyone else and handsome too. From a physical perspective, he's a smart choice. After Samuel anoints him as king, God's Spirit comes upon Saul, and he prophesies. What a promising start for God's first king.

A few days later, Samuel gathers the nation to publicly declare Saul as king. Yet when the time comes, they can't find Saul. He's hiding. We can only guess if he disappears out of fear or if he doesn't want the job. Regardless, his actions suggest that Saul may not turn out to be a good king.

Some time later, Saul gathers his army to fight the Philistines who have come against them. Samuel tells Saul to wait seven days for him so he can come to offer a burnt offering to the Lord and seek his favor. Then Saul can engage in battle.

Saul waits one week, but Samuel doesn't arrive. The army begins to desert, and the king grows anxious. He takes it upon himself to offer the sacrifice.

Just when he finishes, Samuel shows up and rebukes the king for his disobedience. Though God had planned to establish Saul's kingdom forever, God rejects him as king because of Saul's sin, pledging to give the kingdom to another, a man after God's own heart.

Then Samuel anoints David as king. However, David does not ascend to the throne right away, and Saul continues to rule, even though God has left him.

After Samuel dies, Saul is desperate for supernatural guidance, but God is silent. Saul goes to an outlawed medium and asks her to consult the spirit of Samuel. Samuel, irritated at having his idyllic afterlife disturbed, delivers disheartening news to Saul. He prophesies that the Philistines will defeat Israel, with Saul and his sons dying in battle.

This is exactly what happens.

Is our character worthy of what God calls us to do? When God seems distant or remains silent, do we resort to inappropriate spiritual practices?

[Read Saul's story throughout 1 Samuel 9–11, 13–28, and 31. Discover more in 2 Samuel 21:1–14.]

Jonathan (3)

Jonathan is the son of King Saul and next in line to the throne. Though Saul's plan is for Jonathan to succeed him, Jonathan sees God's perspective instead. The heir apparent realizes that David is to be the next king and not him. Jonathan accepts this.

Though there could be animosity between Jonathan and David, the pair enjoy a close relationship, with Jonathan pledging his support for David's future rule.

Another demonstration of Jonathan's character and faith in God comes at a time when Israel's army is outmatched and in despair. Only Saul and Jonathan have swords, while the rest of the army have makeshift weapons.

Jonathan and his armor-bearer sneak away from camp and boldly attack a Philistine outpost. Though Jonathan isn't confident in a victory, he knows God *can* bring it about.

With only one sword, Jonathan and his young armor-bearer kill twenty Philistines. God sends a panic throughout the enemy camp, and they scatter. The Israelite army pursues them and wins a great battle against a more powerful foe.

Through God, one person can make a difference.

Are we willing to accept God's plan for our future when it opposes our families' or friends' expectations? Are we a person God can use to make a difference?

[Read Jonathan's story in 1 Samuel 13–14, 18–20, and 23. Discover more in 1 Samuel 31:2.]

David (1)

David, the shepherd boy turned king, shows up in Scripture more than any other Old Testament character. Even the New Testament mentions him often. He appears in twenty-eight of the Bible's sixty-six books, with more than nine hundred mentions.

It's enough content for an entire book, with much we can learn from David and much God can teach us.

David, however, is best known for two events in his life: one a triumph and the other a failure.

The first story comes from early in his life when he kills the huge warrior Goliath. He takes down this giant of a man using only a slingshot and a single stone. But the projectile doesn't kill Goliath, it only knocks him out. David runs to the fallen Philistine hero and pulls out the man's own sword. David uses it to kill him and then cut off his head.

David's time spent protecting his father's sheep from wild animals prepared him for this moment, but his faith in God gave him the victory.

The other well-known incident in David's life is when he commits adultery with the beautiful Bathsheba.

He sees her. He wants her. He takes her. It doesn't matter that he already has several wives, and she already has a husband.

She gets pregnant.

To cover the pregnancy, David calls back her husband, Uriah, from the front lines and tries twice to reunite him with his wife for the night. When this strategy fails, David sends Uriah back to the front lines along with a message for the commander. The communiqué is a plan to ensure Uriah's death.

The plan succeeds. David marries Bathsheba, but their baby dies.

From a moral perspective, this is the lowest point in David's life. He commits adultery and murder. Yet David repents to restore his relationship with God.

A third element of David's life, however, stands out as even more noteworthy. When Samuel confronts King Saul for his disobedience, Samuel confirms that Saul's kingdom will end, and another will replace him. Samuel says that God has sought a man after his own heart and appointed him to rule the people. This man is David.

Much later, Paul confirms this fact when speaking to the people in Pisidian Antioch, stating that God said, "I've found David, a man after my own heart. He'll do everything I want him to do."

Twice, the Bible refers to David as a man after God's own heart. This may be the highest honor anyone could ever receive.

Are we a person after God's own heart? What might we do to move closer to this outcome?

[Read David's story in 1 Samuel 16 to 2 Samuel 24. Discover more in Acts 13:22.]

Abigail (2)

In the time after Samuel anoints David, but before Bathsheba, David's on the run, hiding from the murderous intent of King Saul. It's at this point that David encounters Abigail.

Abigail is an intelligent, beautiful woman. Her husband, Nabal, lacks these traits. He's surly and mean. His servants call him wicked and say he listens to no one. Abigail agrees. She confirms his name means *fool* and says that folly follows him. Despite this, Nabal is also wealthy, with thousands of goats and sheep.

David and his men decide to protect Nabal's herdsmen and flocks, anticipating he will appreciate their efforts and one day reward them. But Nabal disrespects David's emissaries when they ask for food; he sends them away empty-handed. Boiling with anger, David plans to retaliate. He intends to kill Nabal and his men.

When the astute Abigail hears what happened, she acts without delay. She prepares food for David and his men. She meets his advancing army of four hundred. She humbles herself before him, assumes responsibility (while professing her innocence), wins David over, and stops the massacre.

Abigail confirms that she believes God will provide David with a lasting dynasty. She asks him to remember her when God gives him success. David accepts her words and her provisions. He blesses her.

Nabal roils with anger when he learns what his wife did. He has a stroke and later dies. David receives this news with glee, seeing it as God's vengeance on his behalf. David sends for Abigail so he can marry her. This may be David fulfilling her request when they first met or an honorable act to provide for her.

This takes place while David is on the run, so her new lifestyle is not an easy one. At one point, Abigail is captured, along with the rest of the families of David's men, but he rescues her. She and David have at least one son: Kileab (also called Daniel).

What we best remember about Abigail, however, is the bold action she took to avoid a massacre.

What bold step does God want us to take? How can our actions and our words bring about peace and prevent discord?

[Read Abigail's story in 1 Samuel 25. Discover more in 2 Samuel 3:3 and 1 Chronicles 3:1.]

Bathsheba

Bathsheba is a beautiful woman. Her husband, Uriah, is off fighting in David's army, while the king stays home in the comfort of his royal residence.

From the vantage of his palace rooftop, David sees Bathsheba bathing. He wants her.

Both are at fault. Bathsheba should have been more discreet, and David shouldn't have been looking. David summons her and sleeps with her. He later confesses committing adultery with her. Since adultery is a consensual relationship, this shows she's a willing participant. Given that she bathed in plain view of David's palace rooftop, she may have even been the instigator.

For those who don't want to view Bathsheba as an adulteress, a willing participant in an affair, the other perspective is that she's a victim. In this viewpoint, her rooftop bathing is an innocent act. When David sends for her, she feels powerless to decline the request of a sovereign king and lets him do to her what he wants. It's a sexual assault, a rape. Yet, David doesn't confess to rape but to adultery.

Regardless, Bathsheba becomes pregnant.

Attempting to cover up what happened, David calls Uriah back from the front lines and tries twice to send the soldier home. When that fails, David develops a battle plan that results in Uriah's death. Bathsheba mourns her husband's passing. Then David marries her.

Later, Nathan confronts David for his actions. Once exposed, David acknowledges his mistakes—adultery and murder—and seeks God. However, their child becomes sick and dies.

David and Bathsheba later have Solomon. Solomon eventually becomes king, just as David promised Bathsheba. Centuries later, Jesus is born. He is David and Bathsheba's direct descendant, through Solomon.

What steps should we take to protect us from having an affair? Are we doing all we can to lead a pure, God-honoring life?

[Read Bathsheba's story in 2 Samuel 11–12. Discover more in 1 Kings 1:11–31.]

Uriah (1)

Despite being a foreigner, Uriah the Hittite is loyal to the nation of Israel, to King David, and to God. He's an honorable man, serving in the nation's army.

David stays home while his troops, including Uriah, are off fighting. It's during this time that David sleeps with Uriah's wife, Bathsheba, and she gets pregnant.

To cover up their coupling, David calls Uriah back from the front lines. After two failed attempts to send Uriah home to the arms of his wife, David resorts to plan B. He develops a battle strategy to bring about Uriah's death. Uriah unwittingly carries the plan with him when he returns to the front lines.

The commander implements David's strategy, and Uriah dies.

Uriah is a victim of events outside of his control. He did nothing wrong. Yet he's effectively executed anyway, all because of the king's affair and attempted cover-up.

Though we may view Uriah's life as a tragedy, we should remember him as a devout man of integrity and valor. This is his legacy.

And there's one more thing. Though not an ancestor of Jesus, Uriah's name, nonetheless, appears in Matthew's genealogy of Jesus, whereas his wife's name is absent.

In this way, Scripture honors the admirable Uriah.

When we do what is right, do we expect everything to work out? Will we maintain our trust in God if we suffer unjustly?

[Read Uriah's story in 2 Samuel 11. Discover more in Matthew 1:1–6.]

Mephibosheth

You may remember David's best friend, Jonathan, King Saul's son. Though Saul and all his sons, including Jonathan, die in battle, this doesn't mean his line is wiped out. Saul's grandson, Jonathan's son Mephibosheth, is still alive. The one physical characteristic we know about him is he is lame in both legs due to an accident when he was young.

As a sovereign king, David has the power to kill all members of the former king's family. This would ensure that no heir of the former king remained to try to reclaim the kingdom and overthrow the new ruler.

But King David doesn't follow this practice. In fact, he does the opposite. He seeks out members of Saul's family, not to end their life, but to demonstrate kindness. When he learns of Mephibosheth, he sends for the man.

It's easy to imagine Mephibosheth receiving this summons, no doubt expecting to be executed. He comes before David and bows down in honor. Though this would be the response of anyone called to appear before the king, I suspect Mephibosheth prostrates himself lower, longer, and more reverently than most. He must have assumed this was his last chance at survival and his final act in life.

Instead of ordering Mephibosheth's death, however, David elevates his best friend's son, granting him all his grandfather Saul's land and possessions. David also gives Mephibosheth a place of honor by giving him a permanent seat at the king's table.

David does all this without knowing much about Mephibosheth. The fact that he is Jonathan's son is all David needs to know.

In response to David's generosity, Mephibosheth remains appreciative and loyal to David throughout his life. Mephibosheth continues his commitment to the king even when his servant Ziba lies about him, slanders his reputation, and betrays him.

In all this we see Mephibosheth as an upright man.

What accepted practices should we stop doing to offer a God-honoring alternative? Is there a person we can show kindness to?

[Read Mephibosheth's story in 2 Samuel 4:4; 9:3–13; and 19:24–30.]

Absalom

Absalom is David's third son. Absalom's beautiful sister, Tamar, is raped by their conniving half-brother Amnon. Absalom comforts Tamar and avenges her dishonor by killing Amnon.

Though parents aren't responsible for what their children do, these events suggest David is a hands-off dad who may not have raised his children well or instilled in them a sense of right and wrong. We get implicit confirmation of this when the Bible says David never rebuked another son, Adonijah. It's likely David didn't attempt to correct Absalom or Amnon either.

This may be why Amnon takes advantage of his sister and Absalom takes revenge on Amnon. Rape and murder are not God's way to live. We know this, but Amnon and Absalom don't. Or might they think that as the king's sons they're above the law?

This attitude of doing whatever he wants carries forward in Absalom's life. He wants to become king. With his older brother Amnon out of the way, Absalom now has one less roadblock to achieve his goal.

Absalom doesn't even wait for his father to die. He orchestrates a coup to usurp his father's throne and seize control.

David and his entourage flee for their lives. When Absalom's rebellion falters and David reinserts himself as king, he tells his army to be gentle with his undeserving son. However, Joab, the commander of the army, disregards David's instructions and kills Absalom. This puts an end to Absalom's threat, as well as his sinful behavior.

Have we ever been like Absalom and tried to seize something that wasn't ours? Are we willing to show mercy to a family member or friend who did us wrong?

[Read Absalom's story throughout 2 Samuel 13–18.]

Solomon

After David and Bathsheba's first son dies, the pair later has Solomon. Solomon succeeds his father David as king, though an earlier coup—thankfully unsuccessful—by Absalom nearly kept this from happening. Another brother, Adonijah, also attempts to steal the throne before David makes Solomon king.

As David's successor, Solomon builds the temple his father yearned to construct. Solomon rules well, enjoys peace, and has a reputation for being wise, wiser than anyone else.

Yet for all his wisdom, Solomon makes an unwise decision. It's an action he repeats hundreds of times. He marries foreign women, something the Law of Moses forbids (Deuteronomy 7:3–4). In total, Solomon amasses seven hundred wives and three hundred concubines.

In his old age, his foreign wives turn his attention from the God his father served to the gods they serve. Solomon's heart is divided in loyalty between the one true God and the gods his wives worship.

Though Solomon received a great start in life and ruled with wisdom, his foreign wives distracted him from living a life fully devoted to the Lord, as his father, David, had done. This is a sad ending to an otherwise successful life.

What relationships do we have that may turn our focus away from God? Do we follow all of God's commands or assume, like Solomon, that some don't apply to us?

[Read Solomon's story in 1 Kings 1–11. Discover more in 2 Samuel 12:24 and Nehemiah 13:26.]

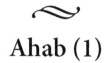

Ahab (1)

After Solomon's reign, the nation of Israel splits into two countries. David's line continues to rule the nation of Judah, while other kings reign over the rest of Israel. Both nations have God as their legacy, but the kings of Israel are consistent in not following him. They rebel and do evil.

One such king, who reigns about a century after David, is Ahab. He's the evilest king of Israel so far. He establishes the worship of foreign gods, Asherah and Baal, instead of God.

He marries Jezebel, a woman even more wicked than himself. Though we can criticize her for her negative influence on her husband, he alone is at fault for what he does.

Ahab begins his twenty-two-year rule as king of Israel while Asa, a good king, reigns in Judah. When Asa dies, his son Jehoshaphat succeeds him. Jehoshaphat is also a God-honoring king like his father.

Though Ahab and Jehoshaphat are opposite from a faith perspective, their nations have a common heritage and a common enemy, the nation of Aram.

When Ahab asks Jehoshaphat to join forces in battle to retake the town of Ramoth Gilead, Jehoshaphat agrees.

But he also wants to seek God's counsel. Ahab's four hundred prophets all predict victory. Jehoshaphat, however, wants input from the Lord's prophets. Ahab knows of one, Micaiah. But the king doesn't like him because the prophet never predicts anything good.

After first sarcastically agreeing with the other four hundred prophets, Micaiah then speaks God's truth. He says Israel will face defeat if they go to battle, and he says Ahab will not return, implying he will die in the skirmish.

Attempting to avoid this, Ahab disguises himself as a chariot soldier so that he won't stand out as a target. But a random arrow hits him, and he dies.

Is there ever a time when we should align ourselves with someone who is evil and doesn't share our faith? When we seek counsel, do we believe the majority opinion or follow the single voice who represents God?

[Read Ahab's story throughout 1 Kings 16–22. Discover more in Micah 6:16.]

Jezebel (1)

A hab, Israel's evilest king so far, marries Jezebel, the daughter of a foreign ruler. Under her influence, Ahab worships her gods instead of the true God. Jezebel also hunts down and kills God's prophets, while providing sanctuary for hundreds of the prophets of Baal and Asherah.

God's prophet Elijah has a public confrontation with the prophets of Baal and Asherah. God and Elijah win, and Elijah kills all the prophets of Baal and Asherah who are present.

In retaliation, Jezebel threatens to kill Elijah. While he's on the run, the queen adds to her crimes. Here's what happens:

Ahab wants a specific vineyard from Naboth because it's near the palace. But Naboth refuses to sell it to Ahab or trade with him. This infuriates the king, but it's Jezebel who acts to get the vineyard for her husband.

She commands the city elders where Naboth lives to gather the people and pay two men to slander Naboth in front of witnesses. They're to testify that

Naboth cursed God (as well as the king) a crime warranting execution.

The city leaders do as she instructed. Then the people stone Naboth to death. Ahab takes possession of the dead man's vineyard.

Eventually, Jezebel suffers a gruesome death. She's tossed from a balcony and stomped to death by horses. This is the price for her evil actions, just as prophesied.

Are we doing everything we can to promote the right worship of God and shun evil? When have we gone too far to do something for a family member or friend?

[Read Jezebel's story in 1 Kings 21:5–23 and 2 Kings 9:7–37. Discover more in 1 Kings 18:4 and 19:1–2.]

Jehoshaphat (3)

Jehoshaphat is the great-great-grandson of King Solomon. Though Solomon's father David ruled well as a man after God's own heart, Solomon's heart was divided and many succeeding kings in their family line did more evil than good.

Jehoshaphat is an exception.

Scripture calls him a good king, just like his father Asa. He follows his father's example and doesn't stray from how his dad raised him.

During Jehoshaphat's twenty-five-year reign, his country, Judah, experiences a time of peace with the nation of Israel. Although Jehoshaphat allies himself with Israel's evil king Ahab in conducting a joint military campaign, God doesn't criticize Jehoshaphat for doing so.

Overall, the Bible characterizes Jehoshaphat as someone who does what is right in God's eyes. Yet this doesn't mean he does everything he should have. No one does.

Despite ruling with wisdom and following God, Jehoshaphat fails to remove the high places where the people go to offer sacrifices and burn incense, contrary to God's command.

Though we could fault Jehoshaphat for this one failure, remember that the Bible characterizes him as doing what is right. This is his legacy.

Do we judge others on what they do right or what they do wrong? As Asa did with Jehoshaphat, what are we doing to train the next generation to follow God?

[Read Jehoshaphat's story in 1 Kings 22. Discover more in Matthew 1:1–8.]

Elijah (2)

Our first encounter with Elijah in Scripture occurs when he goes to King Ahab to warn of a famine-producing drought; no dew or rain will fall until Elijah says so. During this famine, God provides for Elijah, first through ravens at a brook and later through a widow in Zarephath.

After three years of no rain, God sends Elijah back to Ahab. Elijah challenges Ahab's prophets of Baal and Asherah to a spiritual competition of sorts. Elijah and the prophets will each build an altar and pray for fire to rain down from the sky and ignite the offering. The deity who answers will prove he is God.

The 450 prophets of Baal and four hundred prophets of Asherah build their altar and cry out to their gods to send fire. Nothing happens.

Elijah taunts them.

They plead even more, dancing with fervor and mutilating themselves to get their gods' attention. Still, nothing happens.

Now it's Elijah's turn. He builds his altar and arranges the sacrifice on it. Then he drenches everything with water. He prays a simple prayer to

PETER DEHAAN

God—no pleading, dancing, or self-affliction—asking the Almighty to send fire so the people will know he is the one true God.

Fire shoots down from the sky, burning up the sacrifice, the wood, the stones, and the soil around the altar, even consuming the water Elijah poured on everything.

The people bow low in worship, proclaiming the Lord is God.

Instead of joining the celebration, however, Elijah instructs the people to seize the prophets of Baal and Asherah. He executes all 850 of them.

Elijah prays for rain and a downpour occurs.

This would be the perfect place to end our story, but there's more.

When evil Queen Jezebel learns what Elijah did, she threatens to kill him. He runs away in fear.

Yet God doesn't give up on his fickle prophet. He reveals his presence and speaks to Elijah in a quiet whisper. Among other things, God tells him to go and anoint Elisha to succeed him.

Elijah does, and later God takes him up into heaven in a whirlwind. *That's* the end of the story.

Do we have the courage to do what God says even when the odds are against us? Have we ever floundered under the threats of one person, like Elijah did?

[Read Elijah's story in 1 Kings 17–19 and 2 Kings 1–2. Discover more in James 5:17–18.]

Elisha

We earlier saw that Moses appointed Joshua to succeed him. Though preparing someone to carry on our ministry or lead our tribe when we're gone is a wise move, the Bible has too few examples of this occurring. Elijah and Elisha are a noteworthy exception. After Elijah anoints Elisha to succeed him as prophet, he mentors his protégé.

With Elisha trained to take over as God's prophet, both men know Elijah's time on earth is about to end. Elisha insists on staying with his mentor for as long as possible. Elijah asks his protégé if he has any final requests.

He does. He asks to inherit a double portion of Elijah's spirit.

"This is a most difficult request," Elijah says, "but if you see me as I am taken from you, God will provide what you've asked."

They continue walking. Suddenly, a chariot of fire, drawn by horses of fire, appears and separates the two men. Elisha watches Elijah ascend toward heaven in a whirlwind. And that's the last Elisha sees him.

Yet the fact that Elisha sees Elijah as he's taken confirms that God will grant Elisha a double portion of his mentor's spirit.

What a powerful way for him to begin his work for God.

Is there someone we can mentor to continue our ministry when we're gone? Do we live our life in such a way that someone would want to inherit a double portion of our spirit?

[Read Elisha's story throughout 2 Kings 2–8 and 13:14–21.]

Naaman (3)

Naaman is an accomplished military leader for the king of Aram. The Bible calls him a valiant soldier, but he suffers from a limiting physical ailment. He has leprosy. It's a contagious skin disease that can cause a loss of feeling, flesh decay, and even deformation. (You may recall that Miriam contracted leprosy later in her life.)

A band of raiders from Aram make incursions into Israel. They capture a young girl who's forced to work in the household of Naaman. Though she has every right to be bitter about her situation, she tells him of the prophet Elisha, who can heal him of his terrible disease.

Naaman seeks permission from his king to go to Elisha to receive healing. In anticipation of a successful outcome, Naaman prepares gifts to give to the prophet in gratitude. The king of Aram also drafts a letter for the king of Israel, telling *him* to heal Naaman of his leprosy.

The king of Israel is distraught when he reads the letter, knowing he can't heal Naaman, or anyone else, of leprosy. He rips his royal robes in distress, thinking this is an excuse for the king of Aram to pick a fight.

When Elisha hears what happened, he sends a message instructing the king of Israel to send Naaman to him. Yet when Naaman arrives, the prophet doesn't even bother to see him. Instead, Elisha sends a message to Naaman telling him to wash seven times in the Jordan River. This will restore his flesh and take away his leprosy.

Offended that Elisha won't even talk to him and insulted at the instruction to wash in the Jordan River instead of one of the preferable waterways back home, Naaman storms off in a huff. But his attendants encourage him to do exactly what Elisha's message directed.

He does and receives God's healing.

Naaman affirms the power of God and pledges to worship him.

Like Naaman, will we humble ourselves to receive what we want? Do we believe God can heal us today?

[Read Naaman's story in 2 Kings 5. Discover more in Luke 4:27.]

Jonah (1)

Jonah is the best known of the Bible's so-called minor prophets. He runs away from God and spends three days in the belly of a large fish. There he has plenty of time to think about his disobedience to God.

When the fish spits him onto the shore, God speaks to Jonah again. "Go to Nineveh. Once you arrive, I'll give you a message for the people."

This time Jonah obeys, but he doesn't have a good attitude.

We don't know if Jonah says exactly what God tells him to or if he paraphrases it to fit his lack of interest. But what he says is both succinct and blunt. "In forty days, Nineveh will be destroyed."

He doesn't provide correction or offer a hopeful alternative. He states the outcome as fact, providing no instruction for the people to repent. We may wonder how much Jonah cares about the people he preaches to. Or if he even wants them to repent.

He doesn't.

We later learn that Jonah longs to see the destruction of Nineveh. This is because Nineveh is the capital (or principal city) of Assyria, a longtime enemy of Judah and Israel. Surely Jonah and all his people would have cheered to see Assyria fall. They would see this as God's vindication, rescuing them from their adversaries.

It's no wonder Jonah puts little effort into his message.

Despite this, the people of Nineveh believe God will do as Jonah said. They fast. They humble themselves in the hope God may relent and offer them compassion.

Forty days come and forty days go, with Nineveh avoiding the destruction God had planned.

Yet Jonah isn't pleased that the people of Nineveh responded to his message and lived. Instead, our story ends with him complaining to God about his grace. This is the last we hear of Jonah.

When God tells us to do something, do we obey or run away? When we obey God's instructions, do we have a good attitude?

[Read Jonah's story in the book of Jonah. Discover more in Luke 11:29–32.]

Learn more about Jonah in the devotional Bible study *Return to Me: 40 Prophetic Teachings about Unfaithfulness, Punishment, and Hope from the Minor Prophets.*

Athaliah (2)

Athaliah is an evil woman. She encourages her son, the king, to make some ill-advised decisions. He does and is assassinated later. Upon his death, Athaliah seizes control and inserts herself as queen. Her lust for power consumes her, so much that she kills all the members of the royal family, including her own grandchildren.

One baby, however, escapes the queen's execution mandate. This child is Joash. His aunt Jehosheba risks her life to save him from premature death. Six years later, the priest—with the support of the Levites and heads of leading families—crowns Joash, the rightful heir to the throne, as king.

Athaliah flies into a rage. She accuses them of treason. To express her outrage, she rends her clothes. But she can't change what happened. At the direction of the priest, the army kills her.

The country celebrates her death and calm returns.

Athaliah could have positively influenced her son and helped him rule wisely. She could have protected and groomed his successor, one of her grandsons.

Had she done so, the people might have celebrated her life. Instead, they cheered her death.

How might people remember us? Do we do things to help others, or do we only seek to elevate ourselves?

[Read Athaliah's story in 2 Kings 11:1–16.]

Jehosheba

Jehosheba is the daughter of King Jehoram and the sister of King Ahaziah, both kings of Judah. When Ahaziah is murdered, Jehosheba's mother, Athaliah, seizes the throne and proclaims herself as queen, ordering the execution of the royal family—her own family.

At great personal risk, Jehosheba takes bold action to keep her nephew Joash from being killed by his evil grandmother. Jehosheba has little time to consider her actions when she rescues Joash from among the royal princes who are about to be killed.

Jehosheba hides Joash and his nurse in the temple for six years.

When Joash is seven, he's crowned king and his power-hungry grandmother is slain. The people rejoice and peace returns, all because of the boy-king and his aunt who made it possible.

Jehosheba plays a decisive role in protecting the rightful heir to the throne, keeping him alive so that he can one day rule and restore calm to the land.

Sometimes we must react quickly, with only a moment to analyze the situation. May we all be like

PETER DEHAAN

Jehosheba, who acted decisively to do the right thing without concern for her own well-being.

Apart from these two passages that tell of Jehosheba's great valor, the Bible doesn't mention her again. Though she may have lived in seclusion in the temple with her nephew and his nurse, it's quite possible she died along with the rest of her family. She might have sought to save herself first, but she placed a priority on saving her nephew instead, assuring that her brother's legitimate heir would one day rule in his place.

What's something we ought to do, regardless of the risk? Are we willing to face death so that someone else may live?

[Read Jehosheba's story in 2 Kings 11:2 and 2 Chronicles 22:11.]

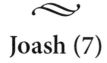

Joash (7)

Young, orphaned Joash lives in the temple for six years, where his nurse cares for him. He's hiding from the queen, his murderous, power-hungry grandmother. The priest is Joash's uncle, Jehoiada, the husband of Jehosheba. We can envision the priest teaching and guiding his young nephew.

When Joash turns seven, Jehoiada anoints the boy as the rightful king of Judah and orders the death of the queen. Though this sounds like a coup, it serves to reestablish the rightful rule by putting the former king's son into power.

Under Jehoiada's influence, Joash rules well.

But after Jehoiada dies, Joash falters. This may be why officials in his court conspire against him and assassinate him. This is a sad legacy to his once-promising start. His son, Amaziah, succeeds him as king.

Though Joash's forty-year reign as king of Judah began well, he didn't finish well.

Are we willing to listen to those who advise us? Is there someone we can guide to make God-honoring decisions?

[Read Joash's story in 2 Kings 11–12.]

Hezekiah (1)

Five generations after Joash, his descendant Hezekiah becomes king of Judah. He's one of the few good ones, perhaps the best. The Bible says he trusts in the Lord God. No king of Judah before or after him is like him. He does right like King David. He removes the high places (which King Jehoshaphat had left) and destroys all the elements of foreign worship, even the bronze snake Moses had made, since the people were burning incense to it.

Scripture says that Hezekiah follows the Law of Moses and enjoys success in all he does.

Yet, despite this, opposition arises.

Sennacherib, the king of Assyria (recall Assyria in the chapter about Jonah), comes with a large army, intent on capturing Jerusalem. Overwhelmed by the size of Sennacherib's force and discouraged by his blasphemous threats, Hezekiah seeks the Lord in desperation, imploring him for deliverance. By miraculously delivering the people, the Almighty would prove he alone is the Lord God.

The prophet Isaiah sends a message to Hezekiah that God will deliver him and the people from Sennacherib's threat. That night an angel of God kills

185,000 Assyrian soldiers. Sennacherib returns home where two of his sons assassinate him.

In this way, God delivers Hezekiah and the people of Judah from a much stronger force. The army of Judah didn't need to do a thing. God rescued them as promised.

Later, Isaiah tells the king to organize his estate, for he will soon die. Distraught, Hezekiah appeals to God in tears, asking the Almighty for a reprieve. That's when Isaiah receives an update from God, a change of plans.

God now promises that Hezekiah will recover from his near-fatal illness and live another fifteen years. Unsure what to think, Hezekiah asks Isaiah for a sign that this will happen. (This reminds us of Gideon's fleece.) Hezekiah's request makes sense because, within a short span of time, Isaiah delivered conflicting messages to the king.

To confirm that the second prophecy supersedes the first, God offers to make the sun travel backward for a time. This will be a sign to Hezekiah that his recovery will take place, just as Isaiah foretold.

The sun does indeed go back, Hezekiah gets better, and the king lives fifteen more years. After Hezekiah's recovery, he writes a psalm of praise to God.

How do we react when we receive conflicting instructions from God? Does our faith remain steady no matter what happens, or does it decrease amid uncertainty?

[Read Hezekiah's story in 2 Kings 18–20. Discover more in Isaiah 38:9–22 and Matthew 1:1–10.]

Isaiah

Isaiah son of Amoz is a faithful and long-serving prophet whose ministry spans the reigns of four kings of Judah: Uzziah, Jotham, Ahaz, and Hezekiah.

Isaiah is the prophet who delivers God's messages to King Hezekiah. The first message promises deliverance from the advancing army. The second is a pair of announcements about Hezekiah's death, with the second one correcting the first.

Does this mean Isaiah got it wrong?

No. Isaiah accurately relays God's message to Hezekiah. But when Hezekiah humbly asks God for a reprieve, the Almighty changes his mind and gives Isaiah the update.

But Isaiah is better known for his amazing prophecies about the coming Savior, the Messiah, which may be why Isaiah is so beloved by followers of Jesus and the most popular of all the prophets in Scripture. This may be in part because he also wrote one of the most cherished of all passages about Jesus:

> For to us a child is born, to us a son is given,
> and the government will be on his shoulders.

> And he will be called Wonderful Counselor, Mighty God, Everlasting Father, Prince of Peace. (Isaiah 9:6 NIV)

New Testament writers either refer to or quote this amazing verse four times, with it showing up in Matthew, Mark, Luke, and Acts. In total, the New Testament references or cites Isaiah's work seventy-nine times, far more than any other prophet. (Only the Psalms garner more New Testament connections, at eighty-one.)

Overall, Isaiah comes in fourth on the list of Old Testament people with the most mentions in the New Testament, coming in after Moses, Abraham, and David.

In addition to Isaiah being a faithful prophet of God with a long ministry, we can applaud him for his impact on the people of his day, the early church, and us now.

What are we doing to impact the people around us? What can we do to encourage future generations?

[Read Isaiah's story in 2 Kings 19–20. Discover more in the book of Isaiah.]

Learn more about Isaiah in the devotional Bible study *For Unto Us: 40 Prophetic Insights about Jesus, Justice, and Gentiles from the Prophet Isaiah.*

Jeremiah (6)

J eremiah, the son of Hilkiah, is both a prophet and a priest. The book of Jeremiah is about the life and ministry of this prophet, but Baruch compiled the content based on Jeremiah's dictation and the scribe's own chronicling of Jeremiah's life. Because of this, we know more about Jeremiah than any of the other prophets who appear in the Bible.

In reading the book of Jeremiah, we see that Jeremiah suffers much for speaking God's word to an unreceptive audience. At various times his detractors threaten him, throw him into a pit, and place him in stocks. More than once, his life is in danger. False prophets oppose and humiliate him. And though he tells the people not to flee to Egypt, they do exactly that and force him to go with them.

One thing unique to Jeremiah's prophecy is that—unlike other prophets—he gives a specific timeline to one of his pronouncements. He says the people will live in exile in Babylon for seventy years (Jeremiah 25:11–12).

Four chapters later, he adds more detail. Jeremiah says that after the seventy years of captivity have passed, God will rescue them, bring them home, and punish Babylon (Jeremiah 29:10).

In the books of Daniel and Ezra, we see this occur just as the prophet proclaimed.

How do we react when people attack and malign us for obeying God? And if we're never persecuted, what does this say about how we live our life?

[Read Jeremiah's story throughout the book of Jeremiah. Discover more in 2 Chronicles 36:21–23 and Daniel 9:2.]

Baruch (1)

Baruch, Jeremiah's faithful scribe and assistant, is the son of Neriah, the son of Mahseiah. Since we know nothing about these two men, they give us little insight into the life of Baruch. All we know about him is what appears in the book of Jeremiah, a document that Baruch wrote most, or all, of at Jeremiah's behest.

In addition to serving as Jeremiah's scribe, Baruch also speaks on the prophet's behalf when he cannot. This puts Baruch in the crosshairs of Jeremiah's detractors. As a result, Baruch also suffers for doing God's work.

The final time we read of Baruch in the book of Jeremiah is Jeremiah's prophetic words about his scribe. Imagine taking dictation for a man of God and then writing down what the Almighty says about *you*. This short instruction from God, through Jeremiah, to Baruch ends with the Lord's promise that wherever Baruch goes, God will let him escape with his life.

The book of Jeremiah notes that when the people flee to Egypt to avoid King Nebuchadnezzar's assaults, they drag both Jeremiah and Baruch with them. But

Baruch later resurfaces in Babylon and prophesies to God's people there. In this we see the fulfillment of Jeremiah's prophecy for his scribe.

Do we think that if we're faithful to God, he will always rescue us? When faced with persecution for obeying our Lord, do we give up or persevere?

[Read Baruch's story in Jeremiah 32:12–16; 36:4–32; 43:1–7; and 45:1–5. Discover more about Baruch's time in Babylon from the apocryphal book of Baruch.]

Ezekiel

Ezekiel is a priest, the son of Buzi. In addition to being a priest, he's also a prophet. He lives in Babylon in exile, the result of King Nebuchadnezzar conquering Judah and deporting most of its people.

The entire book of Ezekiel is about him and by him, but aside from headings added to the Bible, Ezekiel's name only appears twice in his book and nowhere else in all of Scripture. This is because Ezekiel writes in the first person, often using the pronouns *I* and *me*. This makes his writing more personal and accessible.

Instead of using his given name, God often calls Ezekiel "son of man," which occurs ninety-three times in the book of Ezekiel.

This nickname may serve to remind Ezekiel of his humanity, despite being in the priestly line and a prophet of God. Although every one of God's priests, prophets, and servants would be in the same situation, God rarely calls anyone else *son of man*.

As such, we can see *son of man* as a name of affection that God gives his priest-turned-prophet.

This suggests a close relationship between God and Ezekiel.

Ezekiel, as *son of man*, foreshadows Jesus arriving on earth as *the* Son of Man, an even greater affirmation of his close connection with God. Father God sends his son, the Son of Man, to earth to die for us and save us.

If God has a special nickname for us, what might it be? Do we have a close relationship with God, like Ezekiel?

[Read Ezekiel's story throughout the book of Ezekiel.]

PART 5:

DANIEL, PROPHET AND DREAM INTERPRETER

With God's people in captivity, we see him preparing for them to return to the promised land from their exile. But first we must consider Daniel. After him we'll look at the accounts of Ezra, Nehemiah, and Esther. This will wrap up our Old Testament story arc and prepare us for the arrival of Jesus in the New Testament.

Daniel (2)

When King Nebuchadnezzar conquers the nation of Judah, he deports most of its citizens. He sets aside young men who are members of the royal family and nobility. They'll undergo training and be forced into a lifetime of service to the king who conquered them and killed many of their friends and relatives.

Daniel is one of these young men. He may even be a boy when this occurs.

Despite this challenging situation, Daniel and three of his friends pledge to serve God, even though they could have turned their backs on him for not protecting their nation and keeping them safe.

In his work for his captor, Daniel conducts himself well, rising to a level of power and respect. Among other things, he interprets dreams. He also serves at least four kings: Nebuchadnezzar, Belshazzar, Darius, and Cyrus. In all, Daniel's loyal service spans seventy years.

The book of Daniel opens with six stories about him and his three friends. Best known is the account of when his detractors toss him into a pit of hungry lions because of his steadfast worship of God. God protects Daniel throughout the night. The next day he's removed and replaced by his accusers. The hungry lions devour them.

The book of Daniel ends with four prophecies. The third prophecy, as recorded in Daniel 9, happens during the reign of King Darius.

Daniel recalls Jeremiah's prophecy of seventy years of exile before the people return. The time is almost up. Daniel fasts and prays, confessing the sins of the people and imploring God to act. That's when God's prophetic word comes to his prophet. His perspective, prayer of confession, and faith in God are powerful examples for us all to follow.

The Bible says Daniel remains in Babylon until the first year of King Cyrus, and Daniel has another vision two years later.

King Cyrus also allows some of the Israelites to return home. Included in the list of those allowed to return is the brief mention of a man named Daniel (Ezra 8:2). This could be another person with the same name, or it could be this Daniel, who lived in exile for seventy years and returned home in his old age.

Are we willing to be like Daniel and confess the sins of our people? If we're forced to serve people who harmed us, as happened to Daniel, do we still give them our best?

[Read Daniel's story in the book of Daniel.]

Ezra

E zra's ministry begins in the latter part of Daniel's life.

Chronologically, the book of Ezra follows the ending of 2 Chronicles, with 2 Chronicles 36:23 repeated in Ezra 1:2–3. Given this, as well as other clues, some Bible scholars attribute the authorship of 1 and 2 Chronicles to Ezra.

Ezra is a priest and scribe who returns from exile with Zerubbabel to rebuild the temple in Jerusalem. The first six chapters of Ezra give the history behind this momentous development, with Ezra switching to a first-person narrative in Ezra chapters 7–9 when he arrives in Jerusalem to assess the situation.

Ezra is distressed to see that some of the Jews living there have intermarried with those of other religious beliefs, contrary to the Law of Moses. This command isn't to keep the Jewish bloodline pure but to avoid distracting them from God and watering down their faith with contrary religious practices.

Ezra takes his concern to God.

Like Daniel, and later Nehemiah, Ezra prays collectively for the people, confessing their mistakes as a group. He carries their offenses on his shoulders, offering a brief glimpse of what Jesus will later do when he carries all sins, for all people, throughout all time, upon his shoulders, when he dies as the ultimate sacrifice.

Ezra prays, confesses, and weeps. This isn't a private effort, but one done in the open for all to see. In doing so, he attracts attention, and many of the people align with him to address those who disregarded God's commands by marrying outside of their faith.

This brings about repentance, followed by correction. The actions Ezra dictates to fix this problem, however, seem extreme.

The men who married foreign women must send their wives away, along with their children. But these women may not be without fault. Implicitly they have done exactly what God warned against by turning their husbands' attention from the one true God and introducing their foreign religious practices and ideals into their family life.

Although this must be a painful decision for the men who disobeyed God, the effect on their wives and children is much more disturbing. The husbands summarily send these women and their children away to fend for themselves in a society that dismisses single moms, often forcing them to struggle in poverty.

Though this doesn't seem fair, remember that sin carries consequences. Sometimes these consequences affect others.

Which of God's commands are we ignoring? How might our sins hurt others?

[Read Ezra's story in Ezra 7 and 10, along with Nehemiah 8.]

Nehemiah

The events of the book of Nehemiah follow the book of Ezra, with Ezra appearing in the book of Nehemiah and Nehemiah showing up in the book of Ezra. Ezra's task was rebuilding the temple in Jerusalem, whereas Nehemiah focuses on rebuilding the city walls.

Nehemiah's story begins with him in exile, serving King Artaxerxes as cupbearer. Nehemiah's brother returns from Judah and tells Nehemiah the deplorable situation in Jerusalem, with its broken walls and burned gates.

Upon hearing this, Nehemiah sits and cries. He mourns and fasts for several days. He prays to God, confessing his sins and those of his family, along with all God's people, for disobeying the laws of Moses. He ends by asking for favor with the king. Nehemiah is specific, asking God to grant him success that very day.

God, however, delays his response.

Four months later Nehemiah makes a bold appeal to the king to return to Jerusalem and rebuild the city walls. He bravely asks the king to provide resources to make this happen. The king agrees. Nehemiah returns and rebuilds the wall, though not without a bit of drama and severe opposition along the way.

Though Nehemiah led this wall-rebuilding effort with God-honoring wisdom and enjoyed a successful outcome, it all started with prayer and confession.

Do we tend to pray first and then act, or act first and then pray when things don't work out? Are there any sins we should confess for ourselves, our family, or our community?

[Read Nehemiah's story in the book of Nehemiah, especially Nehemiah 2:1–9.]

Sanballat

As Nehemiah sets about rebuilding the wall surrounding the city of Jerusalem, he faces obstacles. These come primarily from three men who band together to oppose him and his work. They are Sanballat, Tobiah, and Geshem. Though they share a common goal to stop Nehemiah, each plays a different role in their efforts to halt the rebuilding of the wall.

First is Sanballat. He's a Horonite, which is likely a race or people group.

Sanballat heads the opposition to Nehemiah and the rebuilding of the wall. Tobiah and Geshem take their lead from Sanballat. Without his leadership, the other two men might not have had the boldness to act against Nehemiah's efforts.

We don't know Sanballat's motivation for obstructing Nehemiah's work, but we do get a hint of it when we later learn that Sanballat's daughter is married to the high priest's grandson. This marriage between a priest and a foreign woman is extra distressing because it occurs not long after Ezra's efforts to eliminate all such unholy marriages.

Perhaps through this alliance, Sanballat enjoys a bit of influence that he fears he might lose under Nehemiah's leadership. This seems a legitimate concern because Nehemiah later drives away Sanballat's son-in-law. Implicitly, this removes Sanballat's connection with the high priest and Jerusalem, lessening his ability to impact what goes on in the temple and in the city.

Have we ever opposed something with selfish motives? Do we use our position to influence God-honoring issues, the matters the Almighty cares about?

[Read Sanballat's story in Nehemiah 2:10–20; 4:1–7; 6:1–14; and 13:28.]

Tobiah (2)

Tobiah the Ammonite is the second of three people who oppose Nehemiah's efforts to rebuild the wall. He takes his lead from Sanballat. At one point we even see Tobiah at Sanballat's side, agreeing with him and speaking against the wall as Nehemiah works to rebuild it.

Later, the pair hires Shemaiah to oppose Nehemiah and intimidate him by claiming there's a death threat against him, attempting to distract him from his work.

Tobiah's main part in the opposition to Nehemiah, however, is that he's receiving intelligence information from the nobles in Judah about Nehemiah and what he is doing. And he is in communication with them, attempting to influence them.

Whereas Sanballat heads up the opposition, we see Tobiah working behind the scenes to gather information and influence the people to advance their agenda.

Like Sanballat, Tobiah is also allied with the Jews through the marriages of both him and his son.

Tobiah even has a room improperly assigned to him in the temple courts.

When Nehemiah initiates his final reforms, the people read from the Law of Moses, which says no Ammonites or Moabites can ever enter the temple (Deuteronomy 23:3). As an Ammonite, this includes Tobiah. He's out.

Have we ever let someone wrongly influence us? Have we ever worked behind the scenes to advance what is right or acted with subversive intent?

[Read Tobiah's story in Nehemiah 2:10; 6:10–19; and 13:1–9.]

Geshem

The final member in the trio of opposition to Nehemiah is Geshem, an Arab.

Once Nehemiah finishes rebuilding the walls, but before he can set the gates, Sanballat and Geshem send Nehemiah a message, imploring him to meet with them.

Nehemiah realizes this is a ploy. He knows they want to hurt him, possibly even kill him, so he declines. Four times they send him this message, and four times he says, "No."

The fifth time, Sanballat and Geshem send Nehemiah the same message via a courier, along with an unsealed letter. In it, they accuse Nehemiah of inciting a revolution and trying to set himself up as king. Sanballat states that Geshem can confirm these charges are true.

In their desperation to stop Nehemiah, Geshem libels him, stating outright lies as truth.

What should we do when others attack our character? What is a God-honoring way to respond when people lie about us?

[Read Geshem's story in Nehemiah 2:19 and 6:1–7.]

Vashti

At this point, some of God's people have returned home from exile, but not all have.

Back in Persia (formerly Babylon) the mighty King Xerxes shows off his wealth, splendor, and majesty to his people for a full 180 days, nearly half a year. Then he gives a weeklong banquet for everyone in the citadel, complete with an open bar.

At the same time, Queen Vashti gives her own celebration, a seven-day party for the women of the palace.

On day seven, an inebriated Xerxes commands the beautiful Vashti to parade herself in front of his drunken guests. The virtuous queen, however, refuses to debase herself before their ogling eyes.

Embarrassed, the enraged ruler asks his advisors what to do. Their answer is quick.

They want to keep other women from following Vashti's example of insubordination and thereby disrespecting their husbands. They fear widespread marital conflict. Therefore, they advise the king to immediately remove Vashti from her position as queen and forever ban her from being in his presence.

With little thought, the king agrees to their proposal. He issues an irrevocable edict and sends Vashti away.

Queen Vashti reacted to the king's degenerate request with chaste virtue. She refused to stoop to his drunken depravity, regardless of the cost. In doing so, she paid a heavy price for her integrity.

This is the last we hear of Vashti in Scripture.

How much value do we place on maintaining our integrity? How much will we risk to do what's right?

[Read Vashti's story in Esther 1:7–20.]

Mordecai (2)

Mordecai is a descendant of the Jews exiled by Nebuchadnezzar when he conquered Judah. Mordecai takes care of Esther, his orphaned niece. In this we see Mordecai as a man of integrity who cares for his relative. He adopts her and treats her like a daughter.

Esther is beautiful, with an attractive figure.

When King Xerxes seeks a replacement for Queen Vashti, Esther is one of the virgins rounded up in the national initiative to find a new queen.

Mordecai instructs Esther to keep her nationality and background secret. We don't know why he does so, but it may be that he fears anti-Semitism from the king's court. Mordecai does what he can to check on his adoptive daughter as she waits in the king's harem.

Around this time, the king elevates one of his advisors, Haman, to a position of high authority. Everyone kneels in honor before Haman, as the king commands, but Mordecai refuses to do so.

Though the Bible doesn't explicitly say it, we can assume Mordecai sees bowing to Haman as being disrespectful toward God, who is the only one deserving his homage.

Mordecai's refusal to bow enrages Haman. He embarks on an extreme revenge campaign, but killing just one Jew isn't enough. To get back at Mordecai, Haman plans to kill all the Jews who live throughout the nation's provinces. He wants to exterminate the entire race.

Mordecai's refusal to bow before Haman could cost him his life—and the lives of all his people.

Are we willing to honor God even if it might result in our death? Will we maintain our integrity even if it puts other people's lives in jeopardy?

[Read Mordecai's story throughout Esther 2–10.]

Esther

After King Xerxes banishes Queen Vashti from his presence, he regrets his rash decision, his irrevocable edict. His aides suggest that he find a replacement. They round up the most beautiful virgins in the land for the king to try out (yes, it's as bad as it sounds). The most pleasing one will be crowned queen.

This isn't a voluntary beauty pageant. It's conscripted service that forces the selected women into a harem. Esther, also called Hadassah, is rounded up in the dragnet. She waits at least four years for her assigned time to spend the evening with the king.

After she sleeps with the king, he proclaims her queen.

When Haman plots the Jews' extermination, Mordecai challenges Esther, his relative and adopted daughter, to intervene with the king on the Jews' behalf. She balks. It's been a month since she's seen the king, and she risks immediate execution by appearing before him without a summons. Mordecai begs Esther to take the risk, saying, "What if God put you in your position to address this exact situation?"

Eventually she agrees. "If I die, then I die," she says.

In preparation, Esther fasts for three days and asks others to fast with her.

When she approaches the king, he spares her life. Instead of directly appealing to him, however, she invites him and Haman to a private banquet with her that night. She then requests they come a second evening. At this second dinner, she reveals Haman's plot, appealing to the king for justice.

Because of her actions, Haman is executed, and the Jews are granted the right to defend themselves and attack their enemies.

The festival of Purim celebrates Esther and her heroics in saving her people.

Though she took time to pray and fast, Esther bravely set her own safety aside and risked her life to save others.

Are we willing to work to save the lives of others even if it puts ours in jeopardy? What risks will we endure to do what's right?

[Read Esther's story in Esther 2–10.]

Hegai

Hegai is not a well-known biblical figure. He's virtually unheard of. His name only shows up four times in Scripture, all in Esther 2. At best, most readers consider him a footnote to Esther's story. But his role may have been pivotal in her quest to find favor with the king.

Hegai, a eunuch, oversees the king's harem of virgins as they await their turn to spend the night with him. Afterward, they join the king's harem of concubines, under the direction of another eunuch.

As she awaits her turn, Esther wins the favor of Hegai. He gives her extra attention and a special place in the harem. When it's her turn to sleep with the king, she seeks Hegai's advice. We don't know what he suggests, but he must have given her wise counsel, for the next day Xerxes proclaims Esther as queen.

Though this outcome is no doubt a result of Esther's actions, let's not dismiss Hegai's role in this. God may have used his sound advice to bring about Esther's success, putting her in position for what happens next.

When people seek our counsel, do we give them the soundest advice we can? Regardless of our job, do we always do our best?

[Read Hegai's story in Esther 2:3–15.]

Haman

Haman is the son of Hammedatha, the Agagite, but the Bible doesn't define what an Agagite is. It could be his race, or it could be a creed he holds. Given Haman's actions, we can wonder if an Agagite is defined by anti-Semitism. Regardless of what Agagite means, we do know that Haman is, in fact, prejudiced.

As the valued advisor of King Xerxes, the king elevates Haman and commands people to kneel before him. Mordecai refuses. In retribution, Haman decides to slaughter Mordecai's entire race—all the Jews.

His plan is thwarted, however, when Esther intervenes for her people. As a result, Haman is executed, along with his ten sons.

Haman should have been pleased when the king elevated him in position and stature. He wasn't. Haman should have been pleased to have people bow in fear and reverence before him. He wasn't.

Haman shouldn't have let Mordecai's attitude disturb him, but he did. His irrational anger and lust for revenge so controlled him that it resulted in his death. In the end he lost his life, along with the position and prestige the king granted him.

When have we been unhappy with what we've had and strived for more? When have we overreacted—in thought or in deed—to a situation or circumstance?

[Read Haman's story throughout Esther 3–9.]

Zeresh

Zeresh is the wife of the anti-Semitic Haman. After Haman complains about Mordecai to his family and friends, Zeresh recommends Haman construct a seventy-five-foot pole and seek the king's permission to impale Mordecai on it. Haman delights in this idea and follows his wife's advice.

His plan is foiled, however, when the king has a different idea. Instead of hearing Haman's plan to execute his nemesis, the king commands Haman to honor Mordecai. After completing this distasteful task, the mortified Haman returns home in humiliation.

Then Zeresh predicts her husband's downfall. Since Mordecai is a Jew, she says, Haman doesn't stand a chance.

She's right.

A few days later, Haman is impaled on the same pole he constructed for Mordecai's execution. Zeresh's initial advice to her husband becomes the tool for his death.

Zeresh gave her husband the guidance he wanted to hear. What if she had counseled him differently, instead encouraging him to rise above his vendetta and not seek revenge?

When we give advice to others, do we offer them the easy answer or the right one? How can we best support our family and friends?

[Read Zeresh's story in Esther 5:9–14 and 6:12–14.]

Jesus

From our perspective today, the purpose of the Old Testament is to point us to Jesus. Though Jesus doesn't appear by name in the Old Testament, he exists throughout its pages.

Jesus is there at creation when God said, "Let us make . . ." (Genesis 1:26; John 1:2, 10; and Colossians 1:15–17).

He is there in the supernatural encounters between God and his people, arriving as the angel of the Lord (Genesis 16:7–11 and over fifty other verses).

And Jesus appears frequently in the prophetic words of God's messengers who look forward to the future Messiah who will come and save the people (such as in Isaiah 9:6–7 and in more than four dozen other passages).

Last, we see Jesus alluded to in the closing chapter of the Old Testament. Malachi foresees the return of the prophet Elijah (Malachi 4:5–6), whom we see personified in John the Baptist (Matthew 17:10–13). John will prepare the people for Jesus's arrival, announcing that he will die for their mistakes and save them (Hebrews 10:10–14).

What a fitting way to conclude the Old Testament.

In what ways has God revealed Jesus to you through the Old Testament? What is your response?

[Read about Jesus's salvation in Luke 1:76–79; John 10:28; Acts 4:11–12; and Ephesians 2:8, as well as throughout the New Testament. Discover more about Jesus in the Old Testament in Isaiah 9:6–7.]

Sinners, Saints, and Us

From a basic understanding, this book considers some of the people in the Old Testament who make mistakes (sinners) and who do good (saints). We can look at their errors to avoid their blunders or to correct our missteps. We can also look at their successes to celebrate what they did well and inspire us to do better.

A more correct understanding of sinners and saints, however, is to acknowledge we are all sinners: every one of us. This includes you and me. As such, we all fall short of God's Old Testament expectations.

Yet Jesus offers us a better way.

When we repent and follow him, he makes us right with Father God, wiping away the penalty our sins deserve and giving us a clean slate. In this way we become saints. This sainthood—our right standing with God—is a gift freely available to anyone who wants to receive it.

All we need to do is accept what Jesus offers. We don't need to change our behavior to gain God's attention or earn our salvation—we can't. It's impossible.

Instead, God has prepared a no-strings-attached present that he graciously offers to us.

It's in *response* to this gift that we seek to change our behavior as a way of saying "thank you" to Jesus for the salvation he has given us.

May the Old Testament characters of the Bible inspire us to move forward as we become more Christlike in response to our salvation. Here are some questions to consider and to spur us on:

- *What Bible character inspired you the most?*
- *Which story surprised you?*
- *What are three errors (sins) you need to repent of and move away from?*
- *What are three errors (sins) you must guard against, so you don't repeat those mistakes?*
- *What three characteristics from these Old Testament people can you celebrate and imitate?*
- *What three characteristics can you aspire to follow so you become more Christlike?*

Contemplate your answers, and seek God to help you move forward. May he bless you as you read his Word and apply it to your life each day. May he receive your efforts as an act of worship, and may the world see your life as a powerful witness.

[Discover more in 2 Timothy 3:16–17].

Bonus Content:

Duplicate Names

Several people covered in this book share their names with other biblical characters. Sometimes these repeated names occur in the same family tree, where the name given to one child is in honor of someone in their lineage. For example, Abraham's grandfather is Nahor (1), and his brother is Nahor (2).

To avoid confusion, I've added a numerical suffix to distinguish duplicates. (Further complicating matters, some of these people also share names with cities or regions.)

Here are the names in this book which are shared with other people in the Bible. Though not always possible, I attempted to list them in chronological order, with the person we covered in italics.

Noah

Noah (1), the man who built the ark (Genesis 6:8–9)

Noah (2), one of the five daughters of Zelophehad (Joshua 17:3)

Eliphaz
Eliphaz (1), the Temanite and friend of Job (Job 2:11)
Eliphaz (2), the son of Esau (Genesis 36:10)

Elihu
Elihu (1), son of Barakel the Buzite and friend of Job
   (Job 32:2)
Elihu (2), the great-grandfather of Samuel (1 Samuel
   1:1–2, 19–20)
Elihu (3), brother of King David (1 Chronicles 27:18)
Elihu (4), one of King David's military leaders, from
   the tribe of Manasseh (1 Chronicles 12:20)
Elihu (5), a descendant of Obed-Edom and implicit-
   ly a gatekeeper for King David (1 Chronicles
   26:7–8)

Sarah
Sarah (1), the wife of Abraham and mother of Isaac
   (Genesis 17:19)
Sarah (2), the wife of Tobias (Tobit 3:7–18 in the
   Apocrypha)

Ishmael
Ishmael (1), the son of Abraham and Hagar (Genesis
   16:11)
Ishmael (2), son of Nethaniah (2 Kings 25:23–25)
Ishmael (3), son of Azel (1 Chronicles 8:38)
Ishmael (4), the father of Zebadiah (2 Chronicles
   19:11)

Ishmael (5), the son of Jehohanan and a commander in Jehoiada's army (2 Chronicles 23:1)

Simeon

Simeon (1), the second son of Jacob and Leah (Genesis 29:33)

Simeon (2), a righteous and devout man in Jerusalem who saw baby Jesus (Luke 2:25–35)

Simeon (3), a prophet and teacher in Antioch; also called Niger (Acts 13:1)

Levi

Levi (1), the third son of Jacob and Leah (Genesis 29:34)

Levi (2), through Joseph, Jesus's great-great-grandfather (Luke 3:23–24)

Levi (3), a tax collector, son of Alphaeus, and follower of Jesus (Mark 2:14)

Tamar

Tamar (1), the daughter-in-law of Judah who gave birth to twins through him (Genesis 38:24–30)

Tamar (2), the daughter of King David, sister of Absalom, and was raped by her brother Amnon (2 Samuel 13:1–22).

Tamar (3), the niece of Tamar (2) and daughter of Absalom (2 Samuel 14:27).

Gad

Gad (1), the son of Jacob and Zilpah; his seventh and her first (Genesis 35:26)

Gad (2), a prophet during the reign of King David (1 Samuel 22:5)

Joseph

Joseph (1), the eleventh son of Jacob and first for Rachel; he was sold as a slave and ended up a ruler in Egypt (Genesis 30:22–24)

Joseph (2), son of Asaph (1 Chronicles 25:2)

Joseph (3), a priest guilty of marrying a foreign wife; a descendant of Binnui (Ezra 10:38–42 and possibly Nehemiah 12:14)

Joseph (4), stepfather of Jesus (Matthew 1:16)

Joseph (5), a half-brother of Jesus (Mark 6:3)

Joseph (6) of Arimathea, a disciple of Jesus and a member of the Council; he buried Jesus (Matthew 27:57; Mark 15:43)

Joseph (7) or Barsabbas, also known as Justus (Acts 1:23)

Joseph (8), a Levite from Cyprus; the apostles call him Barnabas (Acts 4:36)

Benjamin

Benjamin (1), the twelfth son of Jacob and second of Rachel (Genesis 35:24)

Benjamin (2), great-grandson of Benjamin (1) (1 Chronicles 7:6–11)

Miriam

Miriam (1), older sister of Moses and Aaron (Numbers 26:59)

Miriam (2), a child of Mered (1 Chronicles 4:17)

Caleb

Caleb (1), son of Jephunneh, who spied out the promised land for Moses and gave a favorable report (Numbers 13:6, 30)

Caleb (2), son of Hezron (1 Chronicles 2:18)

Joshua

Joshua (1), son of Nun, protégé of and successor to Moses (Exodus 24:13)

Joshua (2), son of Jozadak, and a priest (Ezra 3:2)

Joshua (3), an ancestor of Jesus (Luke 3:29)

Deborah

Deborah (1), nurse of Rebekah (Genesis 35:8)

Deborah (2), a judge and prophet (Judges 4:4)

Deborah (3), the great-grandmother of Tobit (Tobit 1:6–8 in the Apocrypha)

Samuel

Samuel (1), a prophet and son of Elkanah and Hannah (1 Samuel 1:20–21)

Samuel (2), grandson of Issachar (1 Chronicles 7:1–2)

Saul

Saul (1), the first king of Israel (1 Samuel 10:1)

Saul (2), a young Pharisee who initially opposed Jesus's followers before experiencing a dramatic conversion; later called Paul (Acts 9:1–19)

Jonathan
Jonathan (1), a priest, the son of Gershom (Judges 18:30)

Jonathan (2), a descendant of Judah (1 Chronicles 2:32)

Jonathan (3), son of King Saul and friend of David (1 Samuel 14:1)

Jonathan (4), one of David's mighty warriors, the son of Shagee the Hararite (1 Chronicles 11:34)

Jonathan (5), David's nephew, who killed a large man (1 Chronicles 20:6–7)

Jonathan (6), the son of Uzziah, who oversaw some of the king's storehouses (1 Chronicles 27:25)

Jonathan (7), David's uncle (1 Chronicles 27:32)

Jonathan (8), son of Abiathar the priest (1 Kings 1:42)

David
David (1), the second king of Israel, father of Solomon, and ancestor of Jesus (1 Samuel 16:13)

David (2), though this obscure reference could be to King David, given the context, he's likely a different man (Ezra 8:2)

Abigail
Abigail (1), sister of David (1 Chronicles 16–2:13)

Abigail (2), wife of Nabal, who later married David upon her husband's death (1 Samuel 25:39–42)

Abigail (3), daughter of Nahash and sister of Zeruiah the mother of Joab (2 Samuel 17:25)

Uriah

Uriah (1), a loyal soldier of King David and first husband of Bathsheba; known as Uriah the Hittite and one of David's mighty warriors (2 Samuel 11:3)

Uriah (2), a priest during the time of King Ahaz (2 Kings 16:10)

Uriah (3), a prophet, son of Shemaiah from Kiriath Jearim, during the time of King Jehoiakim, who had him killed (Jeremiah 26:20–23)

Uriah (4), a priest during the time of Ezra (Ezra 8:33)

Ahab

Ahab (1), an evil king of Israel (1 Kings 16:29–30)

Ahab (2), a lying prophet during the time of Jeremiah (Jeremiah 29:21–22)

Jezebel

Jezebel (1), the evil wife of King Ahab (1 Kings 19:1–2)

Jezebel (2), a self-proclaimed prophet whom Jesus criticizes in Revelation (Revelation 2:20)

Jehoshaphat

Jehoshaphat (1), son of Ahilud and a recorder during the time of King David (2 Samuel 8:16)

Jehoshaphat (2), one of Solomon's district governors and the son of Paruah from the tribe of Issachar (1 Kings 4:17)

Jehoshaphat (3), a king of Judah, the great-great-grandson of King Solomon, and an ancestor of Jesus (1 Kings 15:24)

Elijah

Elijah (1), a son of Jeroham, likely from the tribe of Benjamin and part of King Saul's family tree (1 Chronicles 8:27)

Elijah (2), a prophet, known as Elijah the Tishbite, during the time of King Ahab (1 Kings 17:1)

Elijah (3), a priest and descendant of Harim who married a foreign wife during the time of Ezra (Ezra 10:21)

Elijah (4), a priest and descendant of Elam who married a foreign wife during the time of Ezra (Ezra 10:26)

Naaman

Naaman (1), a son of Benjamin (Genesis 46:21)

Naaman (2), a descendant of Benjamin and head of one of his clans, possibly the same as Naaman (1) (Numbers 26:40)

Naaman (3), a leper and commander of the army of the king of Aram (2 Kings 5:1)

Athaliah

Athaliah (1), a son of Jeroham (1 Chronicles 8:26–27)

Athaliah (2), an evil woman who killed her royal family so she could seize the throne and become queen of Judah (2 Kings 11:1)

Athaliah (3), a family head and father of Jeshaiah who returned to Judah from exile in Babylon (Ezra 8:7)

Joash

Joash (1), a grandson of Judah (1 Chronicles 4:21–22)

Joash (2), a grandson of Benjamin (1 Chronicles 7:6–8)

Joash (3), father of Gideon (Judges 6:11)

Joash (4), son of Shemaah and one of King David's warriors (1 Chronicles 12:3)

Joash (5), in charge of King David's supplies of olive oil (1 Chronicles 27:28)

Joash (6), a son of King Ahab (2 Chronicles 18:25)

Joash (7), a boy king of Judah and grandson of Athaliah (2 Kings 11:2)

Jonah

Jonah (1), God's unwilling prophet from Gath Hepher, the son of Amittai, who spends three days in the belly of a large fish (Jonah 1:1; 2 Kings 14:25)

Jonah (2), the father of Simon Peter (Matthew 16:17)

Hezekiah

Hezekiah (1), a king of Judah and ancestor of Jesus (2 Kings 18:1 and Matthew 1:1–10)

Hezekiah (2), the great-great-grandfather of the
prophet Zephaniah (Zephaniah 1:1)

Hezekiah (3), listed among the returning exiles
during the time of Ezra and Nehemiah (Ezra
2:16)

Jeremiah

Jeremiah (1), a descendant of Manasseh (1 Chronicles
5:23–24)

Jeremiah (2), one of David's warriors from the tribe
of Benjamin (1 Chronicles 12:2–4)

Jeremiah (3), the fifth of David's warriors from the
tribe of Gad (1 Chronicles 12:10)

Jeremiah (4), the tenth of David's warriors from the
tribe of Gad (1 Chronicles 12:13)

Jeremiah (5), the grandfather of King Jehoahaz
(2 Kings 23:31)

Jeremiah (6), a priest and prophet, the son of Hilkiah
(Jeremiah 1:1)

Jeremiah (7), a signatory of the people's promise (covenant) to observe the Law of Moses
(Nehemiah 10:1–2)

Jeremiah (8), a priest or Levite who returned from
exile with Zerubbabel; he could be the same
person as Jeremiah (7) (Nehemiah 12:1)

Baruch

Baruch (1), Jeremiah's scribe and spokesman
(Jeremiah 36:4–8)

Baruch (2), the son of Zabbai who rebuilt a section of the wall in Jerusalem (Nehemiah 3:20)

Baruch (3), a signatory of the people's promise (covenant) to observe the Law of Moses; he could be the same as Baruch (2) or Baruch (4), but not both (Nehemiah 10:1–6)

Baruch (4), son of Kol-Hozeh who agreed to live in Jerusalem (Nehemiah 11:3–5)

Daniel

Daniel (1), one of King David's sons (1 Chronicles 3:1), also called Kileab (2 Samuel 3:3)

Daniel (2), a member of the royal family or nobility exiled to Babylon. He served under at least four kings: Nebuchadnezzar, Belshazzar, Darius, and Cyrus. He's best known for surviving a night in a den of lions. Though it's a stretch, he could also be Daniel (3) and/or Daniel (4) (Daniel 1:6)

Daniel (3), a family head who returned from exile with Ezra; he could be the same person as Daniel (4) (Ezra 8:1–2)

Daniel (4), a signatory of the people's promise (covenant) to observe the Law of Moses; he could be the same person as Daniel (3) (Nehemiah 10:1–6)

Mordecai

Mordecai (1), an exile who returned to Judah with Zerubbabel (Ezra 2:1–2)

Mordecai (2), Esther's cousin, who raised and adopted her after the death of her parents (Esther 2:7)

Tobiah

Tobiah (1), someone (or the ancestor of someone) who returned to Judah from exile with Zerubbabel (Ezra 2:59–60)

Tobiah (2), an Ammonite official who opposed the rebuilding of the wall in Jerusalem (Nehemiah 2:10)

Aside from duplicate names, some biblical characters have two names (with their better-known name in italics). They are:

- Abram / *Abraham*
- Sarai / *Sarah*
- *Esau* / Edom
- *Jacob* / Israel
- *Joseph* / Zaphenath-Paneah
- *Daniel* / Belteshazzar
- *Esther* / Hadassah

For Small Groups, Sunday Schools, and Classrooms

Old Testament Sinners and Saints makes an ideal discussion guide for small groups, Sunday schools, and classrooms. In preparation for the conversation, read and think about the assigned chapters of this book each week.

When you get together, discuss the questions at the end of each chapter. The leader can either use all the questions to guide your conversation or pick some to focus on.

Before beginning your discussion, pray as a group. Ask for Holy Spirit insight and clarity.

As you contemplate each chapter's questions:

- Look for errors to correct (that is, sins to confess and avoid).
- Consider unwise behaviors and thoughts you should stop.
- Identify God-honoring actions and attitudes you can aspire to.

- Celebrate areas of success and strength to encourage yourself to persevere.

May God speak to you as you use this book to study his Word and grow closer to him.

If You're New to the Bible

Each entry in this book ends with Bible references that can guide you if you want to learn more. If you're not familiar with the Bible, here's an overview to get you started.

First, the Bible is a set of works. Various authors wrote them over several centuries. Think of the Bible as a diverse anthology of godly communication to us. It has historical accounts, poetry, and songs. It also includes letters of instruction and encouragement, messages from God sent through his representatives, and prophecies.

Most versions of the Bible have sixty-six books. They're grouped in two sections: The Old Testament and the New Testament. The Old Testament has thirty-nine books. They precede Jesus and anticipate his arrival. The New Testament has twenty-seven books. They cover Jesus's life and the work of his followers.

The Bible has reference notations, such as Romans 3:23. These resemble line numbers in a Shakespearean play. They serve as a study aid. Since the Bible is much longer and more complex than a play, its reference notations are more involved.

As already mentioned, the Bible presents an amalgam of books, or sections, such as Genesis, Psalms,

John, Acts, or 1 Peter. These are the names given to them, over time, based on the piece's author, audience, or purpose.

In the 1200s, each book was divided into chapters, such as Acts 2 or Psalm 23. In the 1500s, chapters were subdivided into verses, such as John 3:16. Let's use this as an example.

The name of the book (John) is first, followed by the chapter number (3), a colon, and then the verse number (16). Sometimes called a chapter-verse reference notation, this helps people find a specific text with ease, regardless of their version of the Bible.

Here's how to find a passage in the Bible based on its reference: Most Bibles have a table of contents, which gives the page number for the beginning of each book. Start there. Locate the book you want to read, and turn to that section. Next, page forward to the chapter you want. Last, skim the page to find the specific verse.

If you want to read online, pop the entire reference, such as 2 Timothy 3:16, into a search engine. You'll get lots of links to online resources. Or go to BibleGateway.com or use the YouVersion app.

The goal was to place these chapter and verse divisions at logical breaks. But sometimes they seem arbitrary. Therefore, it's good to read what precedes and follows each passage you're studying. The surrounding text may hold relevant insight into the verses you're exploring.

Learn more about the greatest book ever written at ABibleADay.com, which has a Bible blog, summaries of the books of the Bible, a dictionary of Bible terms, Bible reading plans, and other resources.

Acknowledgments

To the God of the Old Testament—and the New—revealed in the Bible. I write for you and to advance your kingdom. May it be so.

To my support network, starting with my wife, Candy, who blesses each day's writing. My assistant, Shara, who does some of my other work so I can write more. My many mentors who teach me from afar about writing and publishing, with Joanna Penn leading them all. My mastermind groups for keeping me moving forward.

To my publishing team, listed in the front of this book: Kathryn, Robyn, and Taryn. You make my work shine.

To my dear friends on my newsletter list. You encourage me, bless me, and motivate me to persevere. You support me in my ministry of words.

And to all who read this book. Though my acknowledgments start with God, they end with you. I write to encourage you in your faith journey and to help you grow closer to God each day. May he bless you throughout your life.

About Peter DeHaan

Peter DeHaan, PhD, wants to change the world one word at a time. His books and blog posts discuss God, the Bible, and church, geared toward spiritual seekers and church dropouts. Many people feel church has let them down, and Peter seeks to encourage them as they search for a place to belong.

But he's not afraid to ask tough questions or make religious people squirm. He's not trying to be provocative. Instead, he seeks truth, even if it makes people uncomfortable. Peter urges Christians to push past the status quo and reexamine how they practice their faith in every part of their lives.

Peter earned his doctorate, awarded with high distinction, from Trinity College of the Bible and Theological Seminary. He lives with his wife in beautiful Southwest Michigan and wrangles crossword puzzles in his spare time.

Peter's a lifelong student of Scripture. He wrote the 700-page website ABibleADay.com to encourage people to explore the Bible, the greatest book ever written. His popular blog, at PeterDeHaan.com, addresses biblical Christianity to build a faith that matters.

Read his blog, receive his newsletter, and learn more at PeterDeHaan.com.

If you liked *Old Testament Sinners and Saints,* please leave a review online. Your review will help others discover this book and encourage them to read it too. That would be amazing.

Thank you.

Peter DeHaan's Books

For the latest list of all Peter's books, go to PeterDeHaan.com/books.

The Dear Theophilus series of devotional Bible studies:
> *That You May Know* (the gospel of Luke)
> *Tongues of Fire* (the book of Acts)
> *For Unto Us* (the prophet Isaiah)
> *Return to Me* (the Minor Prophets)
> *I Hope in Him* (the book of Job)
> *Living Water* (the gospel of John)
> *Love Is Patient* (Paul's letters to the Corinthians)

The 52 Churches series:
> *52 Churches*
> *The 52 Churches Workbook*
> *More Than 52 Churches*
> *The More Than 52 Churches Workbook*
> *Visiting Online Church*

The Bible Bios series:
> *Women of the Bible*
> *The Friends and Foes of Jesus*
> *Old Testament Sinners and Saints*

Other books:
Beyond Psalm 150
Jesus's Broken Church
Bridging the Sacred-Secular Divide
Martin Luther's 95 Theses
How Big Is Your Tent?

Be the first to hear about Peter's new books and receive updates at PeterDeHaan.com/updates.

Printed in Great Britain
by Amazon

43260327R00139